ORIGIN

the story of

CHARLES DARWIN

ORIGIN

the story of

CHARLES DARWIN

Bruno Leone

MORGAN REYNOLDS

PUBLISHING

Greensboro, North Carolina

the

Profiles
IN SCIENCE

series includes biographies about . . .

Nikola Tesla
Louis Pasteur
Tycho Brahe
Johannes Kepler
Nicholas Copernicus
Galileo Galilei
Isaac Newton
Robert Boyle
Rosalind Franklin

Ibn al-Haytham
Edmond Halley
Marie Curie
Caroline Herschel
Thomas Edison
Michael Faraday
Antoine Lavoisier
Charles Darwin

ORIGIN: THE STORY OF CHARLES DARWIN

Copyright © 2009 By Bruno Leone

Library of Congress Cataloging-in-Publication Data

Leone, Bruno, 1939-
  Origin : the story of Charles Darwin / by Bruno Leone.
     p. cm. -- (Profiles in science)
  Includes bibliographical references and index.
  ISBN-13: 978-1-59935-110-0
  ISBN-10: 1-59935-110-2
  1. Darwin, Charles, 1809-1882. 2. Naturalists--England--Biography. I.
Title.
  QH31.D2L395 2009
  576.8'2092--dc22
  [B]
                    2008047204

Printed in the United States of America

First Edition

To Alex, Michael and all the rest

Contents

Charles Darwin *(Courtesy of Getty Images)*

one

An Unlikely Genius

There was nothing about young Charles Darwin that hinted at genius. Except for his boyhood interest in nature, Charles gave little indication that he possessed the talent, resolve, and intellect necessary to become one of the modern world's most influential scientists.

As a student, most school subjects bored him, and his marks were usually mediocre. Hunting, trapping field rats, and collecting natural artifacts captured Charles's attention. These were much more appealing than history, literature, and mathematics.

Charles's father worried that Charles would never have a successful career. He scolded the boy for his lack of interest in school and on one occasion shouted: "You care for nothing but shooting, dogs and rat-catching. You will be a disgrace to yourself and all your family."

Reverend Samuel Butler, headmaster of the public school Charles Darwin attended, once criticized Charles before his entire class, complaining how "this stupid fellow will attend to . . . rubbish but will not work at anything really useful." Later in his life, Charles himself confessed that "when I left the [public school] I was for my age neither high nor low in it; and I believe that I was considered by all my masters and by my Father a very ordinary boy, rather below the common standard in intellect."

No one anticipated that this undisciplined boy would one day revolutionize our understanding of the world. After Darwin completed his life's work, how we view the origin of humankind, its place in the hierarchy of living things, and the role humans will play in the future, was changed forever. More than any other scientist, Darwin redefined how the natural world is viewed.

Charles Robert Darwin was born on February 12, 1809, in the idyllic town of Shrewsbury, England. His father, Robert Waring Darwin, was a successful country doctor; his mother, Susannah Wedgwood Darwin, was the daughter of Josiah Wedgwood, the founder of one of the most famous and respected pottery works in England. Charles was the fifth of six children. There were three older sisters, Marianne, Caroline Sarah, and Susan Elizabeth, and a brother, Erasmus Alvey. The last of the Darwin children, Emily Catherine, was born a year after Charles

Robert Darwin had the most successful medical practice in Shrewsbury. It was rumored his income was larger than any other country doctor in England. In addition to the income from his practice, Robert inherited twenty-five thousand pounds from his father, the physician Erasmus

Charles's father, Robert Darwin *(Courtesy of English Heritage Photo Library)*

Darwin. Charles's maternal grandfather, Josiah Wedgwood, was even wealthier. The Etruscan-style pottery produced in the Wedgwood china plant in Burslem, England, was considered to be the best in Europe. When he died, in addition to his profitable pottery business, Josiah left each of his heirs twenty-five thousand pounds or more.

Charles loved the English countryside near his home. Located on the Severn River, Shrewsbury was a serene rural area situated between two manufacturing areas—Wales to the west and a section of central England called the Midlands.

A potter working at a Wedgwood pottery factory in 1830. *(Courtesy of The Print Collector/Alamy)*

Shrewsbury was untouched by the Industrial Revolution whose factories and wastes were polluting large areas of England.

Shortly after his marriage, Robert Darwin built a two and one half-story red brick house. Named "The Mount" by the newlyweds, the Darwin home sat high on a bluff overlooking a bend in the Severn River

Growing up in the Shrewsbury countryside, Charles was exposed to nature at its finest. The gardens surrounding his home were a colorful patchwork of flowering plants, fruit trees, and shrubs, many of which were unique to the area. His

Charles's childhood home in the English countryside was well away from the pollution and noise of the Industrial Revolution. *(Courtesy of The Print Collector/Alamy)*

mother raised pigeons noted throughout Shrewsbury for their wide variety and beautiful colors. His father, who shared his son's interest in natural history, filled several rooms in The Mount with collections of stuffed animals and old bones. An enormous greenhouse attached to the side of the Darwin home contained plant life both native and foreign to Shrewsbury.

As a child, Charles was an avid collector of everything from rocks to bird's eggs, bugs to minerals and shells. He would attempt to impress family and friends with imaginative stories of his discoveries and accomplishments and invented tall tales about exotic birds he had seen, or about how he had developed a method for changing the color of flowers. While this enthusiasm for nature was typical of many children his age, Charles's appreciation deepened as he grew older. By the summer of 1819, his urge to collect specimens had become a lifelong commitment. During a vacation that year on the Welsh coast with his sisters Marianne and Caroline, Charles wandered off day after day to hunt insects, seashells, and other natural artifacts. Returning to his hotel room, he would study and catalogue his daily finds, and even attempt to determine their biological classifications.

Many years later, when Charles was a student at Cambridge University, his passion for nature and collecting moved beyond being simply a hobby. It developed to the point of becoming an obsession. Later, he recalled one incident, in which, "on tearing off some old bark [from a tree], I saw two rare beetles and seized one in each hand; then I saw a third and new kind, which I could not bear to lose, so that I popped the one which I held in my right hand into my mouth. Alas it ejected some intensely acrid fluid, which burnt my tongue so that I was forced to spit the beetle out, which was lost, as well as the third one."

Unfortunately, no one, including Charles, knew where his interest in nature would lead. It seemed that his interests were at best a chronic distraction and at worst a guarantee for failure. As for Charles, he was happiest outdoors, searching and collecting.

Like most middle-class English children of the nineteenth century, Charles Darwin's schooling began in the home. The responsibility of tutoring Charles fell upon his sister Caroline. His only classmate was his younger sister Catherine, who, according to Charles, was a much faster learner. In the spring of 1817, at age eight, he was enrolled for one year in a day school run by the local Unitarian minister, Reverend George Case.

During these years, Charles's education was mostly informal and consisted of learning the basics of reading and writing,

Charles and his sister, Catherine, in 1816 *(Courtesy of English Heritage Photo Library)*

as well as good manners. His more formal education started in the summer of 1818 when he entered the Shrewsbury Grammar School. His time at the School amounted to little more than seven disappointing and frustrating years for Charles. Headmaster Samuel Butler, a pedantic classical scholar who tended to be overly demanding and uncompromising, ran the school. The curriculum was composed primarily of the works of ancient Greek and Roman authors. It was necessary for Charles to learn Latin and Greek so that he would be able to do his reading assignments in the original languages. A smattering of ancient history and geography were also required. These subjects were of no interest to Charles.

To get through the curriculum, Charles frequently copied assignments off of friends and habitually studied in carefully measured increments so as to get by with the minimal amount needed to pass examinations.

There was, at least, one positive side to attending the Shrewsbury school. It was located within one mile of Charles's home. Although he was a boarder at the school, he was able to run home regularly to be near his family and rummage through his beloved collections of rocks and minerals.

On the whole, though, the years Charles spent at Reverend Butler's institution were discouraging. Charles wrote that "the school as a means of education to me was simply a blank." On June 17, 1825, one year before he was scheduled to complete his studies, Robert Darwin decided that Charles should withdraw from the school. Recognizing that his son was accomplishing very little there and was interested even less, Dr. Darwin concluded that changing schools was the best possible solution.

Charles and his father agreed that he would continue his studies at the University of Edinburgh Medical School. Medicine was becoming a Darwin family tradition. Both Robert Darwin and Robert's father Erasmus were doctors. Charles's brother Erasmus had just completed three years of medical studies at Cambridge University and was planning to complete his final year of studies at Edinburgh. So all parties involved, including Charles, decided that he should follow the family custom. He was interested in science, after all, and medicine would provide a respectable scientific career.

The University of Edinburgh

As a way of testing Charles's ability and interest, Robert Darwin had Charles spend the summer of 1825 working as his medical assistant. Charles accompanied his father on his rounds, consulting with Dr. Darwin about each patient's condition and possible treatment. On occasion, his father even allowed him to prepare a patient's medication. Charles impressed his father, passing his tests. Dr. Darwin was convinced that Charles had succeeded in winning the confidence of each of the patients they visited, and that his son would be able to earn a good living as a physician. As for Charles, he claimed to have "a keen interest in the work." So in October, Charles enrolled in the University of Edinburgh Medical School—considered at the time to be the best medical school in England.

Unfortunately, after entering the University, Charles decided that medical studies were as tedious as the classical studies at

Erasmus Darwin, Charles's paternal grandfather, was a physician and natural philosopher. *(Courtesy of The London Art Archive/Alamy)*

the Shrewsbury school. "The instruction at Edinburgh was altogether by Lectures, and these were intolerably dull," he wrote. Charles specifically recalled two of his professors to illustrate his point. One was Dr. Duncan whose "lectures on Materia Medica at 8 o'clock on a winter's morning are something fearful to remember." The other was Dr. Monro, an anatomy professor, who "made his lectures on human anatomy as dull as he was himself."

Charles faced an even greater problem: he discovered that he simply did not have the stomach for medical practice. Several of the more serious cases he saw during visits to the clinical wards in the university hospital distressed him so much he was haunted by their memory for years. He had to witness two operations performed without chloroform or any other anesthesia. The pain and suffering of the patients being operated upon sickened him so much that he refused to attend any more operations.

Charles managed to stay in medical school for two full years. When he could bear it no longer, he discussed his dissatisfaction with medicine and the University of Edinburgh with his sisters, who in turn informed their father. Once again, Robert Darwin had to face the prospect of directing Charles toward a suitable school and career. Charles's interest remained in nature, but degrees in the natural sciences were not offered at any of the universities in England. Law, medicine, philosophy, and theology were the more common areas of study. Universities did offer courses in many of the sciences, as well as literature, history, and languages. But by and large, classes in these areas were offered for personal enrichment. If Charles was set on devoting his life to natural history, it would have to be as a leisure activity, not as a vocation.

With few options left, Robert Darwin suggested that Charles enroll in Cambridge University and study for the ministry. As a clergyman, Charles would have a respected profession and still have enough time to pursue his interest in nature. He might even be assigned a rural parish, where the countryside would provide him with a surplus of insects, vegetation, streams, and wildlife of every variety.

Charles wasn't sure the ministry was the right choice, and told his father he needed some time to consider it. As he later wrote: "I had scruples about declaring my belief in all the dogmas of the Church of England [Anglican Church]." He decided to read books dealing with the creed of the Anglican Church and the existence of a supreme being. This soul-searching helped convince him of "the strict and literal truth of every word in the Bible" and to conclude that the Anglican "creed must be fully accepted."

Charles agreed to pursue his theological studies at Christ's College, one of the many colleges comprising Cambridge University. If all went according to plan, he would earn a bachelor of arts degree in three years and be ordained a minister shortly thereafter.

However, before Charles could formally enroll at Christ's College as a divinity student, he had a major obstacle to overcome. Cambridge required all divinity students to be able to translate parts of the Bible from Greek to English, which meant knowledge of the ancient language was necessary. But in the two years since he left Shrewsbury school, Charles knowledge of Greek had deteriorated. "I had actually forgotten, incredible as it may appear, almost everything which I had learnt even to some few of the Greek letters," he wrote. However, after several months of study with a private tutor, Charles was able to relearn what he'd forgotten, and could translate the Greek poet Homer as well as New Testament Greek.

Early in January 1828, Charles Darwin arrived at Cambridge to begin his theological studies. He was confident that he had finally discovered the area of study that would lead to his future career. An exciting new start was waiting for him at the end of his three years at Cambridge. But it wasn't what Charles or his family expected.

two

The Making of a Scientist

C ambridge University, one of England's leading institutions of higher learning, was founded when a group of disgruntled scholars migrated there from Oxford, another English university. Angered because their classes had been suspended by the administration at Oxford, in 1209 the scholars banded together and organized their own school.

As a university, Cambridge remained somewhat unimportant until the early 1500s when a divinity school was established. From that point on, the university began attracting prominent professors from England and the rest of Europe, including the noted Dutch philosopher Desiderius Erasmus. It was in 1669 that Cambridge became one of the preeminent universities of Europe. In that year Isaac Newton, the legendary scientist and mathematician, became professor of mathematics. Newton held the position for thirty years and was

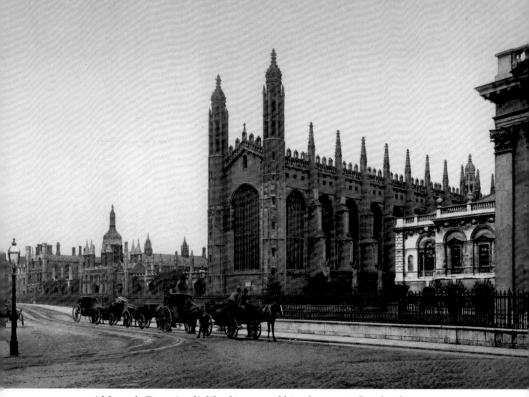

Although Darwin disliked many of his classes at Cambridge University in England, he later referred to his time there as happy and fulfilling. *(Library of Congress)*

largely responsible for elevating the institution to one of the world's leading centers for the study of mathematics. When Charles Darwin decided to enter Cambridge, the university's reputation was well established.

Darwin's education at Cambridge mirrored his earlier school experiences. He wrote that "during the three years which I spent at Cambridge my time was wasted, as far as the academical studies were concerned, as completely as at Edinburgh and at school [Shrewsbury]." He disliked mathematics, which he referred to as "repugnant." He still found ancient classical studies disagreeable and attended only a handful of required lectures. He only applied himself when he had to study for exams during his second and third years at the university.

The one required subject Darwin did enjoy was theology. The works of Reverend William Paley (1743-1805), an Anglican theologian, especially fascinated him. Paley's area of specialty was natural theology, a blending of science and religion. According to Paley and other natural theologians, the perfection, order, and complexity evident in the natural world is evidence of a supreme creator. Two of William Paley's books, *Evidences of Christianity* and *Moral Philosophy*, were required reading for all divinity students at Cambridge. When Darwin first read Paley, he was particularly impressed by the logic he used to prove that the hand of God is evident in nature. Darwin paid Paley a compliment when he wrote years later in his *Autobiography*: "The careful study of [Paley's] works, without attempting to learn any part by rote, was the only part of the Academical Course which, as I then felt and as I still believe, was of the least use to me in the education of my mind."

Though Darwin didn't like most of his classes, Cambridge proved to be a positive experience. Later in life, he referred to those years at the university as his happiest and most fulfilling. During his three years at Cambridge, his long-held love of nature focused into an interest in science. Slowly and steadily, Darwin began maturing into a genuine scientist. He spent much of his spare time in the countryside surrounding the university seeking, collecting, and cataloging whatever specimens he could find. Whenever possible, he enrolled in one or more of the science courses offered at Cambridge. Moreover, Darwin met many people, both fellow students and faculty, who shared his passion for science.

One person particularly inspiring to Darwin was John Stevens Henslow, a good-natured and knowledgeable professor of botany. Charles Darwin and John Henslow had much in common. Like Darwin, Henslow was born into a very prosperous professional family, and as a boy he had collected everything from insects to minerals. Like Robert Darwin, Henslow's father insisted that his son pursue a career as a clergyman and sent him to Cambridge. Soon, Henslow became sidetracked by science. He took courses in chemistry and mineralogy, and upon graduation at age twenty-six, became a professor of mineralogy at Cambridge. One year after his academic appointment, he was ordained a minister and appointed pastor of Little St. Mary's Church near the university's Botanic Garden.

Soon after his ordination, Henslow was appointed Regius Professor of Botany. The man who previously had held the position was not a botanist, had not lectured on botany for more than thirty years, and no longer lived at the university. This was not an unusual situation: at both Oxford and Cambridge Universities, professorial positions in sciences such as anatomy, chemistry, mineralogy, geology, and botany by and large were considered honorary. A professor was paid for the position but was not required to lecture. However by the time Henslow received his appointment, many science professors had begun taking their assignments more seriously.

Henslow proved to be one of the new breed of science professor, and he approached his appointment with immense enthusiasm and determination. He planned a restoration of the university's botanic garden, which had fallen to disrepair under his predecessor. The garden was moved from its location near St. Mary's Church to a conservatory on the

John Henslow, a professor of botany at Cambridge, became a mentor to Darwin. *(Courtesy of The Print Collector/Alamy)*

outskirts of Cambridge. Henslow offered botany lectures and laboratory sessions in the new facility on a routine basis. He also announced that field trips into the countryside around Cambridge to study the area's plant life would be available to all interested students. Most of Henslow's science colleagues shared his enthusiasm, progressive attitude, and competence.

Darwin first heard about Henslow from his brother Erasmus. As a medical student at Cambridge several years before Charles entered the university, Erasmus took courses from Henslow and was impressed by the professor's grasp of virtually every branch of science. On his brother's recommendation, Charles began attending Henslow's botany lectures shortly after arriving at Cambridge and continued attending until graduation three years later. The depth and clarity of Henslow's presentations stimulated him. He also appreciated how the professor "used to take his pupils, including several of the older members of the University, [on] field excursions, on foot, or in coaches to distant places, or in a barge down the river, and lectured on the rarer plants or animals which were observed. These excursions were delightful." Studying nature in the wild under the guidance of Henslow would prove invaluable to Darwin when he himself later traveled around the world as a naturalist.

Every Friday evening during the school term, Henslow invited all undergraduate students who were interested in science to his home. Darwin always attended. The discussions at these gatherings were lively and informative, usually centering upon subjects such as chemistry, mineralogy, geology, botany, and entomology. Many senior faculty members were also regular attendees at the weekly sessions. These meetings gave Darwin the opportunity to hear "the great men of those days, conversing on all sorts of subjects, with the most varied and brilliant powers."

Darwin was in awe of his teacher, Henslow. In his *Autobiography*, he complimented Henslow's deep religious convictions, his knowledge of science, and his modesty. He even referred to Henslow as "the most perfect man I ever met."

Henslow himself was impressed by Darwin's enthusiasm for natural history, and the two grew closer.

In addition to the weekly Friday night sessions, Darwin frequently was invited to the Henslow home for dinner. Darwin and Henslow went on long walks where they would converse on a broad range of topics from science to theology to contemporary politics. When Darwin had to take his final exams in January 1831, it was Henslow who tutored him in the academic areas that he found difficult—philosophy, mathematics, and history. The deepening relationship between the two men did not go unnoticed by either students or faculty at Cambridge: Darwin was often referred to as "the man who walks with Henslow."

Henslow introduced Darwin to the inner circle of scientists at Cambridge. In fact, it was during Henslow's Friday night socials that Darwin became acquainted with many of the university's other resident scientists, most notably Adam Sedgwick and William Whewell.

Adam Sedgwick was a professor of geology at Cambridge, a position he held for more than fifty years. As a scientist, his reputation exceeded even Henslow's. Although Sedgwick was largely self-taught, there were few that could equal his knowledge of geology. In 1831, he was elected Fellow of the Royal Society (an organization of England's leading scientists) and president of the Geological Society of London.

Sedgwick's particular strength as a geologist was his dedication to correct fieldwork. When he first received his appointment as professor of geology, he had had no experience as a practicing geologist. To demonstrate his commitment to his new position, he allegedly said: "Hitherto I have never turned a stone; henceforth I will leave no stone unturned." More so

Adam Sedgwick introduced Darwin to practical fieldwork in geology, during which Darwin learned of the connection between geology and natural science.

than any other geologist at Cambridge, Sedgwick regularly went on geological digs throughout England and continental Europe. At John Henslow's instigation, it was Sedgwick who first introduced Darwin to practical fieldwork. And more importantly, it was through Sedgwick that Darwin came to appreciate the importance of geology for anyone seriously interested in natural science.

William Whewell began his teaching career at Cambridge as a lecturer in mathematics, and was appointed professor of mineralogy in 1825 when Henslow gave up the position to assume the botany professorship. Like Sedgwick, he was a fellow of the Royal Society and widely admired. But unlike Sedgwick, his interests were without boundaries. A child prodigy, Whewell blossomed into a Renaissance man whose tastes and abilities ranged from moral philosophy to church architecture. He was accomplished in astronomy, physics, geology, economics, philology, and a host of other academic areas. Darwin admired Whewell and learned much during his association with him. He noted that "Dr. Whewell was one of the older and distinguished men who sometimes visited Henslow, and on several occasions I walked home with him at night. Next to Sir J. Mackintosh [a philosopher and historian who was related by marriage to Darwin's uncle, Josiah Wedgwood] he was the best converser on grave subjects to whom I ever listened."

During his final year at Cambridge, two books Darwin read enriched his understanding of science and nature, and helped to shape his own scientific philosophy. The first was a work by John Herschel entitled *Preliminary Discourse on the Study of Natural Philosophy*. Herschel, a noted astronomer, wrote the *Discourse* to serve as a blueprint illuminating the techniques of modern science. Herschel believed that there are laws governing all of nature. He explained with great clarity that although these laws are not always obvious or easy to ferret out, they are discoverable by induction (the process of determining general principles from particular facts). Discovering these laws is essential since they provide the very foundation upon which natural science rests. The book also contained Herschel's notion that through science, society could and

John Herschel

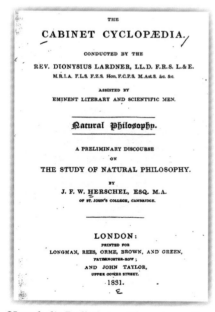

Herschel's *Preliminary Discourse on the Study of Natural Philosophy* enhanced Darwin's understanding of natural laws.

would eventually achieve material progress and well being.

The second publication, written by Alexander von Humboldt, was much different from the Herschel book. Humboldt was a geologist and world traveler. He kept detailed notes of his travels and discoveries, publishing them in a six-volume epic called *Personal Narrative of Travels to the Equinoctial Regions of the New Continent*. The work contained not only scientific information uncovered at the sites Humboldt visited, but also exciting stories of everything he encountered from the native populations to spectacular sunrises and sunsets. Humboldt's work had an immediate impact upon Darwin. Years later in a letter to a friend Darwin wrote that he believed Humboldt was "the greatest scientific traveler who ever lived."

An illustration from a 1807 book by Alexander von Humboldt depicting him and his party collecting specimens in South America. *(Courtesy of The Natural History Museum/Alamy)*

Darwin claimed that Herschel and Humboldt's books "stirred up in me a burning zeal to add even the most humble contribution to the noble structure of Natural Science." Later in his life, when he was preparing his own theory for publication, Darwin made certain that the content of his book reflected the standards and methods Herschel and Humboldt adhered to in their own works.

In January 1831, Darwin was scheduled to take his final exam at Cambridge. The exam consisted of a series of written tests in theology, philosophy, mathematics, and physics spread over a three-day period. He remained at school during the

Christmas holidays in order to cram for his upcoming test—if he didn't pass every part of the exams, he wouldn't graduate. Given his academic record at the Shrewsbury School and the University of Edinburgh, he was not particularly confident. However, his hard work paid off: of the 178 degree applicants who passed their exams, Darwin ranked tenth. All that remained before he was allowed to graduate was to fulfill the university residency requirement by completing the academic year at Cambridge.

In June 1831, Darwin returned home to Shrewsbury with his degree from Cambridge. He planned to seek ordination as an Anglican minister and situate himself in a country parish. Before settling into his planned career, though, he planned a brief holiday. Cambridge geologist Adam Sedgwick had arranged a geological dig in North Wales beginning in August and at John Henslow's request, agreed to have Darwin accompany him.

For most of August, Darwin and Sedgwick scoured the hills and valleys of Wales, studying and cataloging their geological finds. The trip and the work he did with Sedgwick made Darwin realize "that science consists in grouping facts so that general laws or conclusions may be drawn from them."

After his expedition with Sedgwick ended, Darwin returned to Shrewsbury on August 29, though he expected to remain there for no more than a few days. He planned to depart for a second holiday, partridge hunting with his family and friends at Maer, the estate of his uncle Josiah Wedgwood. But when he arrived home, his father handed him a letter postmarked London.

The letter was from Darwin's friend and mentor, John Henslow. An English ship, HMS *Beagle*, was scheduled to embark on a two-year expedition around the world. The ship's captain, Robert FitzRoy, was looking for someone to travel on board as the ship's naturalist. FitzRoy had contacted George Peacock, a professor of astronomy at Cambridge who recommended Henslow. Since Henslow was not willing to leave his wife for so long a period of time, he declined the offer. Instead, Henslow proposed that his former student Charles Darwin go in his place.

Darwin was elated by the proposal. On such a voyage, he would have the chance to learn and experience more about natural history than he could in a lifetime of study in England. For a young naturalist, it was ideal.

But Darwin had one major obstacle to overcome before he could accept. He had to convince his father to allow him to go, and Darwin was certain that would be nearly impossible.

three
Aboard the
Beagle

By nineteenth-century standards, the HMS *Beagle* was a small ship. Built in 1820, it was only ninety feet long and twenty-four feet wide at midship. The *Beagle*'s size, however, did provide it with certain advantages. Unlike larger ships, it could maneuver well in restricted waterways and, when necessary, be towed in and out of narrow and confined harbors by oarsmen in large rowboats. The *Beagle* was therefore an ideal boat with which to chart unknown waters—precisely what the British Navy planned for it.

Eight years after its maiden voyage, Robert FitzRoy, a young and promising British naval officer, was made captain of the *Beagle*. Under FitzRoy's command, the *Beagle* completed two of its most successful assignments, charting the eastern and western coastlines, harbors, and estuaries of South America. The British Admiralty then decided that the ship, with FitzRoy at its helm, was ready for more ambitious

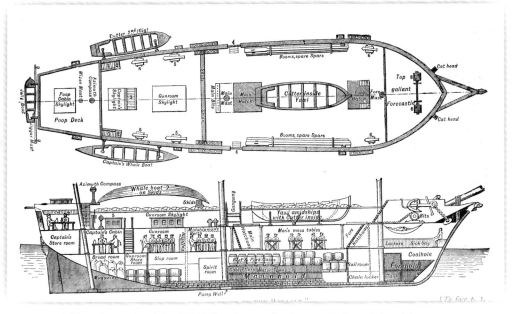

This schematic of the HMS *Beagle* reveals the small size of the ship.
(Courtesy of The Natural History Museum/Alamy)

things. It scheduled the *Beagle* to embark upon a two-year voyage during which it would not only survey coastal South America but also circumnavigate the world.

Before that was possible, however, the *Beagle* was in desperate need of an overhaul. Among other problems, a large section of the ship's hull was rotting away and needed replacing. So in the summer of 1831, the *Beagle* sailed into harbor at the port city of Plymouth, England, to undergo repairs. Shortly after docking, Captain FitzRoy contacted Professor George Peacock at Cambridge requesting his help in locating a naturalist to sail with the ship on its upcoming global voyage.

Since the eighteenth century, having a naturalist on board a surveying ship was a customary practice in the British Navy.

A trained naturalist was qualified to identify most varieties of plant and animal life, collect specimens, and help to determine their usefulness, if any. More importantly, a naturalist with training in geology could possibly discover the presence of precious stones and valuable minerals. All of this was of enormous value to a naval power like Great Britain, which was building a worldwide colonial empire.

Captain FitzRoy also had personal reasons for wanting a naturalist on board the *Beagle*. He was seeking a traveling companion, someone to talk to. Specifically, he wanted an educated, well-bred gentleman with whom he could dine daily and exchange ideas. Since it was considered improper for a ship's captain to socialize with members of his crew, a fellow traveler would be the only one available to help relieve the loneliness and boredom of the extended sea voyage. The *Beagle*'s previous captain committed suicide during a fit of depression off the coast of South America. Since FitzRoy himself also suffered from bouts of depression, he was afraid of being alone for long periods of time.

Charles Darwin was ideally suited for the position. He was not only a gifted naturalist, but also everything FitzRoy was seeking in a companion: young, intelligent, eager, refined, friendly, agreeable, and an attentive listener. However when Charles informed his father of the offer to sail on the *Beagle*, the elder Darwin refused to give his support. Robert Darwin saw no good in a two-year voyage, and presented his son with what he felt certain were eight powerful objections. The objections ranged from his worries that the trip would be "disreputable to [Charles'] character as a Clergyman," to his final assertion that "it would be a useless undertaking."

Robert FitzRoy, captain of the HMS *Beagle (Courtesy of The London Art Archive/Alamy)*

Since his father's approval was essential, Charles felt that he had no choice but to decline the offer. On August 30, he mailed Henslow a letter informing him of his decision. In it, Darwin wrote that "if it had not been for my father I would have taken all risks. . . . I am very much obliged for the trouble you have had about it; there certainly could not have been a

Darwin as a young man *(Courtesy of Getty Images)*

better opportunity." The following day he left for Maer and the start of the partridge-hunting season.

As soon as he arrived at Maer, Charles told his Uncle Josiah Wedgwood about the offer to sail on the *Beagle* and his father's refusal to grant permission. Josiah told his nephew that he thought it would be wise for him to accept the offer. He volunteered to try to persuade Charles's father to change his mind. He wrote a letter to Robert, stating: "The undertaking would be useless as regards his profession [a clergyman], but looking upon him [Charles] as a man of enlarged curiosity, it affords him such an opportunity of seeing men and things as happens to few."

Despite his "eight objections," Darwin's father had told his son, "If you can find any man of common sense, who advises you to go, I will give my consent." Robert had always considered Josiah Wedgwood to be sensible, so had no choice but to give his son his blessing. Charles immediately wrote John Henslow, and was relieved to hear that the post was still available.

On September 5, Darwin traveled to London to meet with Captain FitzRoy. Although FitzRoy was impressed by Darwin's recommendations, at the time he was seriously considering another candidate. However after a series of meetings, FitzRoy began leaning toward Darwin. Darwin's conversational skills, pleasant manners, and personal interests particularly impressed him. On September 11, FitzRoy invited Darwin to sail from London to Plymouth to inspect the *Beagle*. Soon after arriving in Plymouth, FitzRoy officially offered Darwin the position.

For the next three months, Darwin impatiently waited in Plymouth while the sailing was repeatedly delayed. The *Beagle* was supposed to leave in early October. Repairs, however, were proceeding at a slower pace, and several last-minute decisions to upgrade some of the ship's equipment contributed to the delay. Darwin began developing anxieties, complaining to friends of heart palpitations, loneliness, and the gloomy weather. He referred to those three months in

Plymouth as "the most miserable which I ever spent." It was not until December that FitzRoy finally declared the vessel seaworthy.

Then, beginning on December 10, there were several attempts at departure. With each attempt, however, the ship was forced to return to port due to heavy weather. Finally, on December 27, 1831, HMS *Beagle* sailed out of Plymouth harbor into the English Channel headed for South America.

Shortly before setting sail, Darwin received a letter from Henslow, suggesting that Darwin bring along a copy of a recently published book by Charles Lyell, a Scottish geologist. Released in July 1830, *Principles of Geology* was the first of a three-volume series. Henslow, who recognized the importance of geology to a naturalist like Darwin, suggested that it would be a valuable aid on Darwin's voyage.

Charles Lyell was a lawyer who abandoned the legal profession in 1827 to devote all of his time to geology. He had developed a deep interest in the science when, as a student at Exeter College at Oxford University, he attended lectures by William Buckland, one of the early pioneers in the science. Buckland's lectures so impressed Lyell that he began spending much of his spare time on geological field studies. He graduated with honors from Oxford with a bachelor of arts in December 1819, and moved to London to study law. During this time in London, he continued his field trips which in time developed into a passion for geology. When Lyell decided to give up law in 1827 his reputation as a geologist was rising, and with the publication of the *Principles of Geology*, he became known as one of Europe's foremost geologists.

The *Principles of Geology* is considered the most influential book ever written on the subject of geology. One reason

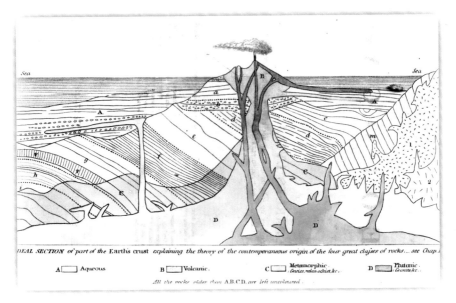

IDEAL SECTION of part of the Earth's crust explaining the theory of the contemporaneous origin of the four great classes of rocks... see Chap.

A ☐ Aqueous   B ☐ Volcanic.   C ☐ Metamorphic. Gneiss, mica-schist, &c.   D ☐ Plutonic. Granite &c.

All the rocks older than A.B.C.D. are left uncoloured.

An image from Lyell's *Principles of Geology,* (second American edition, 1857), showing the origins of different rock types.

is that in *Principles*, Lyell develops the concept of uniformitarianism, which has become the foundation of modern geology. Although he was not the first geologist to propose this theory, Lyell's presentation was the most comprehensive and convincing explanation available.

Prior to the publication of Lyell's book, most geologists were advocates of catastrophism, a theory which argued that the physical appearance of the earth was the result of sudden and unexpected catastrophic occurrences such as floods, fires, and widespread volcanic eruptions. These periodic catastrophes were responsible for the differing geological formations which characterize the earth. Between these disastrous episodes were eras of relative calm with little or no geologic activity taking place. William Buckland, Lyell's teacher at Oxford, was a rigid supporter of catastrophism.

The theory of uniformitarianism was a refutation of catastrophism. It is based on the idea that the geological history of the earth, as detailed by Lyell, is a continuous, uninterrupted succession of physical events directed in the past by the same laws which govern them in the present. Lyell argued that the forces of nature at work today are identical to those active throughout history and prehistory. Moreover, those same forces occur continuously in a measured, stable, and predictable manner.

Lyell concluded that mountains, rivers, valleys, lakes, deserts, and their like did not appear after a sudden and dramatic creation. Rather, they were formed in a gradual, "uniform" fashion, the results of natural forces at work over hundreds of thousands and perhaps millions of years. Rivers slowly cut and shaped canyons; the uplifting brought on by underground volcanic activity created mountains; colossal shifts in the earth's crust were responsible for the formation of continents; and the decaying parts of dead plants and animals along with endless deposits of inorganic materials brought by wind and rain helped form the countless layers of strata found throughout the earth.

Lyell's hypothesis pointed in only one, inflexible direction: the earth is in a gradual yet constant state of flux and has been so since the beginning. This notion had a strong impact on Darwin's thinking.

With Lyell's book in tow, Charles Darwin sailed off for his journey aboard the Beagle. Though he had been optimistic about the trip, he soon discovered the voyage would not be without hardships. From nearly the first day the *Beagle* left Plymouth, he encountered something he had not anticipated: seasickness. When the ship was rocked by inclement weather and violent seas, Darwin became so ill that he was forced to retire to his cabin for days at a time. In a letter to his father mailed from Brazil on February 8, 1832, he described the hardship of life at sea in turbulent waters:

> The misery I [have] endured from sea-sickness is far beyond what I ever guessed at . . . Nobody who has only been to sea for twenty-four hours has a right to say that seasickness is even uncomfortable. The real misery only begins when you are so exhausted that a little exertion makes a feeling of faintness come on. I found nothing but lying in my hammock did me any good.

Darwin did not recover from his first bout of seasickness until January 6, 1832, when the *Beagle* sailed into the harbor at Tenerife in the Canary Islands. During his entire time sailing aboard the *Beagle*, not a month went by without Darwin spending several days and sometimes weeks suffering from seasickness.

Making things more difficult, Captain FitzRoy's attitude and behavior proved to be frequently unpleasant. When Darwin first met FitzRoy, his warmth and kindness impressed Darwin. Shortly after their initial meeting, he referred to FitzRoy in a letter to Henslow as "everything that is delightful. If I was to praise half so much as I feel inclined," he continued, "you would say it was absurd, only once seeing him." He also mentioned FitzRoy in a letter to his sister Susan declaring that "It is no use attempting to praise him as much as I feel inclined to do, for you would not believe me. One thing I am certain, nothing could be more open and kind than he was to me."

But once at sea, another side of FitzRoy's personality suddenly surfaced. The captain's behavior became unpredictable, and he began having repeated and oppressive mood swings. He would become domineering, critical, unreasonable, assertive, complaining, and quick-tempered. Then for no apparent reason, FitzRoy would lapse into forbidding silences that seemed to threaten the crew nearly as much as his explosive states. Darwin learned that the crew secretly referred to the captain as "hot coffee" because of his inclination to boil over.

Still, FitzRoy's erratic behavior did not result in his being detested by either Darwin or his crew. On the contrary, he was mostly respected. FitzRoy was an extremely competent and confident sailor who could be relied upon to safely guide the *Beagle* through all various dangers, and everyone aboard the ship respected him. During those periods when FitzRoy's more agreeable aspects surfaced, he was charming and courteous.

Despite the seasickness, Captain FitzRoy's occasional outbursts, and some scattered misadventures, the voyage of the *Beagle* was the most meaningful event of Darwin's life. He later vowed that he would always regard the date the *Beagle* sailed out of Plymouth Harbor as the birthday of his second life. As his uncle Josiah had pointed out, the worldwide journey exposed him to places and persons very few would ever be privileged to experience. And the discoveries he made as the ship's naturalist eventually would pave the way for his groundbreaking work.

four

A Voyage of Discovery

The voyage of HMS *Beagle* was originally planned as a two-year naval operation. The ship was scheduled to explore the eastern and western coastlines of South America as well as off-shore island groups. Then the *Beagle* was to sail westward into the South Pacific, across the Indian Ocean and around the southern tip of Africa. Short stopovers in Tahiti, New Zealand, Australia, and South Africa were planned, before the ship would head for its final destination, Falmouth, England. However, the voyage took three years longer than originally planned since the ship came upon large sections of the South American coastline which were either unknown to the English navy or difficult to navigate. On numerous occasions, the *Beagle* found it necessary to crisscross earlier routes and revisit areas it had already explored. The coastlines of Argentina and Chile alone took nearly three years to survey.

The slow pace of the *Beagle*'s explorations ultimately worked to Darwin's advantage. On numerous occasions he was able to leave the ship and spend weeks at a time on shore as the ship moved with deliberateness back and forth along the coast. It was at these times that he began taking notes and collecting specimens that would eventually provide the basis for many of the books and monographs he would later write.

Darwin collected thousands of specimens. He took insects, rocks, birds, plants, and fossilized bones he found buried in the dirt and rock. Darwin kept a few specimens aboard the *Beagle* for his personal study, but the majority were shipped back to Reverend Henslow at Cambridge University along with letters detailing his views on the samples and where and how he found them. Darwin requested that Henslow distribute the collection among other scientists for their analyses and opinions. Among those with whom Henslow shared the collection were anatomist Richard Owen, and ornithologist John Gould. When he later returned to England, both men would be of great importance to Darwin.

During much of the voyage of the *Beagle*, Darwin focused primarily upon geological observations. From his earliest introduction to geology, Darwin, like most members of the scientific community, subscribed to the theory of catastrophism. Catastrophists assumed that after each catastrophic upheaval, various life forms would reappear anew and thrive safely until the next catastrophe occurred.

Throughout the lengthy voyage, Darwin found substantial evidence to challenge this widely held geological theory. For example on January 16, 1832, the *Beagle* set anchor at Santiago in the Cape Verde Islands, its first stop. From the ship, Darwin observed a cliff facing the shoreline. Later, as

Richard Owen

he scaled the precipice, he discovered a horizontal band of white shells embedded in the cliff nearly fifty feet above sea level. Darwin theorized that the band of shells had been at sea level at one time, and probably was raised following some underground seismic activity.

To his great surprise, however, the shells were mostly intact. He realized that a sudden and powerful eruption in the earth resulting in the uplifting of the entire band of shells surely would have caused the shells to break. Also, it was unlikely that the layer in which the shells were embedded would have remained uniformly horizontal after such a force. The only explanation lay in Lyell's theory of uniformitarianism—large-scale geological events like the one he was observing tend to occur gradually, not in any sudden or catastrophic manner.

In April 1834, Darwin, along with several ship's officers and about twenty crew members boarded three small whaling boats to explore the Santa Cruz river valley in southern Argentina. The valley ranged from five to ten miles in width, and the cliffs on either side of the valley rose to a plateau more than three hundred feet above the river.

Darwin noticed that the walls of the valley contained layers of unbroken shells virtually identical to those he had seen in similar situations and at similar levels throughout South America. He also discovered intact shells and other exam-

While exploring the Santa Cruz river valley, Darwin noticed that the walls of the valley contained layers of unbroken shells and other sea life. *(Courtesy of WorldFoto/Alamy)*

ples of sea life scattered on the plateau. Catastrophism could not explain how the intact shells ended up atop the plateau, so Darwin explained this phenomenon with Lyell's theory of uniformitarianism. Little by little over time, the plateau, and probably the entire Andes mountain range which ran the length of South America, had been raised from the ocean floor.

As Darwin explored the places visited by the *Beagle*, he observed the native life forms, recording his observations in his journal and collecting precious specimens. He showed an interest not only in the physical characteristics of the individual species he saw but also in their relationship to one another.

He was intrigued by the animals and plants he frequently encountered which, though obviously related, showed clear differences in one or more significant respects. For example, Darwin collected mice living on both the Atlantic and Pacific sides of the Andes Mountains. He was able to identify thirteen species native to the Atlantic side and five native to the Pacific. What he found most interesting was that in terms of size, shape, and other identifying physical characteristics, those inhabiting the Atlantic region were noticeably different from the Pacific species.

In September 1835, the *Beagle* sailed to the Galapagos Islands for a five-week stay. Located off the northwest coast of equatorial South America, the Galapagos are a chain of thirteen major and six smaller islands with a total land area of 3,093 square miles. The plant and animal life Darwin found on the various islands was very different from what was found elsewhere in his travels, but what really interested him was that each individual island contained plants and animals unique to that island. In 1839 when he first published his

A view of the Galapagos Islands, where Darwin made many of his most important observations. *(Courtesy of The National Oceanic and Atmospheric Administration)*

Journal of Researches (now referred to as the *Voyage of the Beagle*) Darwin wrote:

> The natural history of these islands is eminently curious, and well deserves attention. Most of the organic productions are aboriginal creations, found nowhere else; there is even a difference between the inhabitants of the different islands. . . . The archipelago is a little world within itself.

The individuality of the islands first became evident to Darwin when he observed the giant tortoises living there. Although very similar in size, the shapes and patterns of the shells of the tortoises varied widely. Darwin later learned from the vice-governor of the Galapagos that he, the vice-governor, could determine which island a particular tortoise inhabited simply by studying its shell.

Darwin noticed that the shells of the giant tortoises of the Galapagos varied from island to island. *(Courtesy of The National Oceanic and Atmospheric Administration)*

Darwin also observed the birds of the Galapagos. He identified several different types of mockingbirds and an even larger variety of finches on the islands. Each variety of bird inhabited a different island, and each was well adapted to life on its particular island. For example, one species of finch had a curved, thin beak which it used to avoid cactus spines as it removed insects from holes in the plant. Darwin found the curved-beaked finches on an island with a large number of native cacti.

Whenever Darwin visited an island or island group during his voyage, he discovered that the life forms native to those islands bore a more striking resemblance to similar species living on nearby continents than to those living in more distant lands. The finches of the Galapagos, for example, more closely resembled the finches of South America than they did those of Africa, England, or anywhere else. This was true of all life forms.

Some time after returning to England, Darwin was able to see the connection between each of his observations and the theory of uniformitarianism. The changes in mountains, canyons, oceans, and other natural barriers would, over vast periods of time, isolate a species of plant or animal from its original parent. Once separated by a mountain or isolated on an island that species would adapt to ecological and climatic conditions in its new home. It would gradually undergo physical modifications which helped it carry on in its new environment. The influence of Charles Lyell and the theory of uniformitarianism upon Darwin were immeasurable. Darwin wrote that on the Cape Verde Islands, the first stop of the *Beagle*, he was convinced "of the infinite superiority of Lyell's views over those advocated in any other works known to me." Lyell's insistence that nature was undergoing continual and gradual change provided the foundation for natural selection, the unique component of

While studying the different birds of the Galapagos, Darwin discovered that each species was adapted to life on its particular island.

Darwin's theory of evolution. Darwin carried Lyell's theory into the living world by speculating that as the environment in which a species lives undergoes change, so must that species adapt to those changes if it is to survive.

Later in his life Darwin wrote: "I always feel as if my books came half out of Lyell's brain, and that I have never acknowledged this sufficiently . . . I have always thought that the great merit of the Principles [of Geology] was that it altered the whole tone of one's mind."

Despite his discoveries and the pleasure he took in his work, the long voyage was taking its toll on Darwin. He was homesick after five years away from his country and loved ones. He began showing signs of melancholia at least two years before returning to England. In July 1834, while on the west coast of South America, he received a letter from his sister Catherine containing a note written by a mutual friend. He immediately wrote his sister that reading the note made him wish the voyage was over. On February 14, 1836, in Hobart Town on the island of Tasmania, Darwin wrote to his family, stating that he was prepared to board the next ship he saw going directly to England; he stayed aboard the *Beagle*, though, committed to his duty.

In May of 1836, the ship docked for two weeks at the Cape of Good Hope in South Africa. There, Darwin was invited to the home of John Herschel, the author of *Preliminary Discourse on the Study of Natural Philosophy*, a book Darwin greatly admired. "I felt a high reverence for J. Herschel, and was delighted to dine with him at his charming house at the C[ape] of Good Hope," Darwin wrote. "He never talked much, but every word which he uttered was worth listening to."

In June 1836, as the voyage was nearing its end, the *Beagle* began heading north after leaving Cape Town on the southern tip of Africa. Captain FitzRoy insisted on retracing the route the ship followed when it first left port. This would take the Beagle back to the east coast of South America and add several weeks to the passage home. In August, Darwin wrote his sister Susan that the captain's "zigzag manner of proceeding is very grievous; it has put the finishing stroke to my feelings. . . . I loathe, I abhor the sea and all ships which sail on it."

On October 2, 1836, nearly five years after leaving, the *Beagle* arrived in Falmouth, England. Darwin traveled the additional 250 miles to Shrewsbury by coach. He arrived late on the evening of October 4 and found his family asleep. Exhausted, he went to bed as well. The next morning, Darwin's father and sisters were already at breakfast when their Darwin walked into the dining room. The normally reserved Darwins were joyful at their reunion.

The voyage of the *Beagle* was behind him, and Darwin was facing an important decision: What he was going to do with the rest of his life?

five

The Return Home

B efore the voyage of the *Beagle*, Darwin had planned to be ordained as an Anglican priest. But during his explorations abroad, Darwin realized that he could never become a clergyman.

Two reasons lay behind this realization. The first was science related. When he agreed to sail on the *Beagle*, Darwin believed that the voyage would be an opportunity to gather plant and animal specimens from exotic places few Europeans would ever see. But during the voyage, he found more specimens than he anticipated, many of which were very unusual. Not content to merely catalog them, he began wondering about the specimens himself, and he observed connections and patterns between the many finds. He began feeling a strong satisfaction in his scientific work, realizing that science should be his career and not just a hobby.

During Darwin's journey, he also began to have doubts about his faith. For example, Darwin acknowledged that certain species had, from time to time, become extinct. The fossil remains that he found of animals no longer in existence were proof of this. Before his voyage, Darwin, like most catastrophists, believed that after each extinction God created other animals to take the place of the extinct.

The fossil remains of extinct animals he found during his voyage led Darwin to question the theory of catastrophism.

The observations Darwin made on the Galapagos Islands and elsewhere contradicted these previously held convictions. Inspired by the uniformitarian idea that Earth is and always was in a state of continual change, Darwin theorized that species of plants and animals could also be transformed. The transformation would occur over many millennia as changing environments pressured certain species to adapt to new conditions. Plants and animals that did not adapt would become extinct, and those that kept adapting would evolve generations later into different species better suited for life in their new surroundings. Darwin realized that in his new theory, the changes perhaps occurred by chance, and were not necessarily the work of the divine.

In addition to Darwin's own doubts about becoming a priest, by the time he returned from his voyage he had already gained some repute among England's scientists. John Henslow had forwarded the collections Darwin sent from South America—along with the detailed notes Darwin included with the specimens—to England's most prestigious scientists and institutions. Even Darwin's father Robert, who had been so reluctant to allow his son to take the job as naturalist aboard the *Beagle* was convinced that his son should be a scientist. While Darwin was still at sea, his father was visited by Adam Sedwick, who assured him that Charles would one day take his place among the world's "leading scientific men." Later, when Robert Darwin learned of his son's decision to pursue a career in science, he arranged for him to receive a steady income.

Ready to begin a career in science, Darwin spent nearly two weeks with his family in Shrewsbury, then traveled to Cambridge and met with Henslow on October 15.

Darwin and Henslow discussed what would be done with the large collection of Darwin's specimens still aboard the *Beagle*.

A week later, Darwin traveled to London for a reunion with his brother Erasmus. While in London, he planned to take delivery of his specimens, which were due to arrive from Falmouth. He visited the city's museums looking for scientists and others who might be interested in examining, cataloguing, and housing his collection. On October 29, the same day his specimens arrived from Falmouth, Darwin was invited to dine at the home of Charles Lyell. It was the first time the two had met. Darwin had been surprised to learn that the famed geologist was as interested in meeting him as he was in meeting Lyell. The mutual admiration in time grew into a deep friendship which was to last the rest of their lives. Also present that evening was Richard Owen, one of England's foremost zoologists and anatomists. Owen had received many of Darwin's specimens (from Henslow) and wanted to meet Darwin as well.

The three men discussed the distribution of what remained of Darwin's specimens. Lyell promised to help Darwin place as many as possible in the hands of interested and competent naturalists. Owen, who had recently been appointed Hunterian Professor at the Royal College of Surgeons in London, agreed to take the fossil collection. The rest were parceled out among various scientists as well as the British Museum and the Zoological Society of London's Museum.

On December 13, Darwin moved to Cambridge. He liked Cambridge and had always felt comfortable there. Moreover, he would be living among Henslow and many other like-minded scientists. After spending nearly a week

Charles Lyell

at the Henslow home, he moved into his own quarters near the university.

By March 1837, however, Darwin had become disenchanted with his old college town. It now seemed small and provincial, and he realized that it was not a breeding ground of contemporary scientific ideas. Despite his aversion to noise, soot, and overpopulation, he decided to move to London. London, he reluctantly concluded, was the focal point of scientific activity in England and the best place for professional growth and recognition. Not only did most notable scientists reside in London, but also most of England's scientific organizations and societies were headquartered there.

Once in London, Darwin lived with Erasmus for a brief time before moving into his own apartment on Great Marlborough Street, just a few doors from his brother's flat. Although he disliked London and felt it was smoky and dirty, his years in the capital city were very productive. Shortly after his move he began writing a book entitled *The Zoology of HMS Beagle* for which he received a one-thousand-pound government grant (The *Zoology* took him more than six years to complete). Also during 1837, Darwin had five papers published, each related to his experiences and discoveries while on the *Beagle*.

In 1838, he was admitted to membership in the Royal Geographical Society, elected vice president of the Entomological Society, and secretary of the Geological Society. In January of the following year he was made a fellow of the prestigious Royal Society.

In 1839, Darwin published his first book, *Journal of Researches into the Geology and Natural History of the Various Countries Visited by HMS Beagle*, a 200,000-word account of his five-year voyage. The *Journal of Researches* was an instant success, bringing Darwin worldwide recognition. He was especially thrilled by the highly enthusiastic congratulatory letter he received from German naturalist and explorer Alexander von Humboldt. In addition to Lyell's *Principles of Geology*, von Humboldt's *Personal Narrative of Travels* was the only other work Darwin brought aboard the HMS *Beagle*, and he called the work an unmatchable standard in the genre of scientific travel memoirs.

The *Journal of Researches* was released in America as *The Voyage of the Beagle*, the title it's known by today. While its

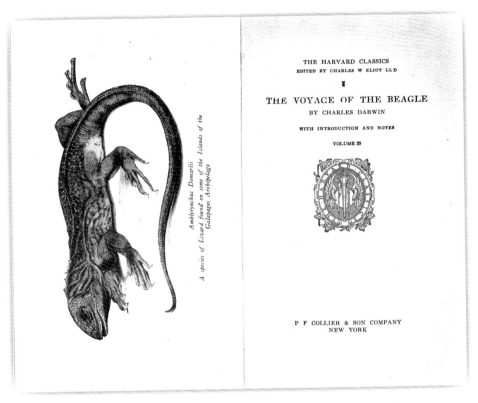

THE HARVARD CLASSICS
EDITED BY CHARLES W ELIOT LL D

THE VOYAGE OF THE BEAGLE
BY CHARLES DARWIN

WITH INTRODUCTION AND NOTES

VOLUME 29

P F COLLIER & SON COMPANY
NEW YORK

A species of Lizard found on some of the Islands of the Galapagos Archipelago

Amblyrynchus Demarlii

The frontispiece of an American edition of *The Voyage of the Beagle,* Darwin's first book.

impact and notoriety never compared to the later *Origin of Species* published in 1859, the published account of his world voyage remained special to him. "The success of my first literary child always tickles my vanity more than that of any of my other books," he wrote later.

While living in London, Darwin was frequently visited by his cousin Emma Wedgwood. He had known her his entire life, but during her trips to London his feelings for her began to deepen. He considered marrying her, but with typical reserve, Darwin did not allow his emotions to carry him blindly into a lifelong commitment like matrimony.

Emma Wedgwood *(Courtesy of The London Art Archive/Alamy)*

Instead, he drew up a list of items weighing the pros and cons of marriage. On a scrap of blue paper he created two columns labeling one "Marry" and the other "Not Marry." In the "Marry" column, he listed things like children, companionship, someone to care for his home, and help insure he remain in good health. The second column was filled with objections such as loss of personal freedom, higher daily expenses, less money for books, and the need to visit relatives.

In the end, he decided to marry Emma. Darwin sought and received the approval of his father for the prospective union. During the summer of 1838, he traveled to Maer Hall, the Wedgwood estate, and began to seriously court Emma. The following November, he proposed to her, much to the delight of everyone in the Wedgwood and Darwin families.

Since both families were affluent, arrangements were made to insure the comforts of the couple. Emma's father, Josiah Wedgwood II, offered a 5,000-pound dowry and an annual stipend of four hundred pounds. Dr. Robert Darwin agreed to invest 10,000 pounds on the couple's behalf in addition to a five-hundred-pound gift every year. Between the money received from their fathers and the royalties Darwin would receive from sales of his books, the couple's financial future was secure.

Charles and Emma were wed at the Wedgwood church, Saint Peter's, on the afternoon of January 29, 1839. That evening, the couple boarded a train for London to begin their married life in a house they had rented on Upper Gower Street. Named Macaw Cottage because of its parrotlike color scheme, Darwin had been living there alone for nearly a month before the wedding, and his books and specimen collection were already scattered around.

Darwin with his eldest son, William, in 1842. *(Courtesy of English Heritage Photo Library)*

The Darwin marriage was a happy one. Emma gave birth to ten children, four girls and six boys. Three of those children did not survive though: Anne Elizabeth, Charles Waring, and Mary Eleanor. Anne's death in 1851 was especially trying for the Darwins as the ten-year-old girl suffered through an agonizing and lingering illness caused, it is believed, by a breakdown in her autoimmune system. "Tears still sometimes come into my eyes, when I think of her sweet ways," Darwin wrote of Anne. Her suffering and death furthered weakened Darwin's already shaken religious faith.

Darwin's movement away from traditional Christian beliefs was one of the few significant issues that occasionally caused conflict with Emma. Emma was a devout Christian who literally accepted most of the biblical teachings with which she was raised. She became troubled over the direction her husband's research was taking, and his growing belief that life was governed by nature's laws, not God's intervention.

Darwin was well aware of his wife's fears. Whenever he discussed his theories with Emma she would voice her objections, frequently asking him to reconsider the course he was taking. But neither his wife nor anyone else could persuade him against moving ahead. He was driven onward by a growing belief that life and the natural history of the world was not what most scientists of his day portrayed. Nor was it what Christian philosopher William Paley had proposed in 1802 in his widely read book *Natural Theology: Evidences of the Existence and Attributes of the Deity, collected from the Appearances of Nature.* The more Darwin researched the subject, the more he came to believe in his own developing theory of biological evolution.

six

The Theory of Evolution

The concept of evolution predated Charles Darwin by more than two millennia. The sixth and fifth century BCE Greek philosophers Anaximander and Empedocles both claimed that the earth and all things inhabiting it are in a state of constant flux and development. The Roman philosopher Lucretius (first century BCE), although best known for his theory that all matter is composed of countless atoms, offered an explanation not only for the continual presence of change in the natural world but also for the origin of life itself.

During the Middle Ages, some Islamic and Christian thinkers believed that God created all things, and that He instilled His creation with a large enough supply of energy to insure it would undergo continual transformations. Throughout most of history, however, advocates of what modern science specifically refer to as evolution faced unyielding opposition and remained in a very small minority. It was not until Europe's scientific revolution in the sixteenth and seventeenth centuries that the theory of evolution began gaining an increasing number of determined supporters to challenge, if not match, its equally vocal detractors.

The scientific revolution was a key moment in Western history. It was an intellectually fertile period when several generations of creative thinkers applied new methods of study to explore the mysteries of the physical and biological worlds. Critical thinking and objective experimentation replaced the blind acceptance of ancient and medieval authorities. This unbiased approach to learning obligated philosophers and scientists to question and sometimes completely revise flawed ideas and assumptions dating from previous eras in science.

As a result, major advances began taking place in disciplines like physics, astronomy, anatomy, embryology, mathematics, mechanics, medicine, chemistry, optics, and other related areas. Moreover, new areas of study emerged, some of which directly threatened teachings long held sacred by most scientists and theologians. Geology was one such discipline.

Geology is the science which investigates the composition and history of the physical earth and the countless life forms which have inhabited it. Geologists teach that much can be learned from studying the earth's rock formations or strata. The existence of ancient oceans, rivers and lakes, unrecorded global warmings or frosts, the presence of prehistoric terrestrial and aquatic life—all of these and more could be studied and understood through the study of Earth's crust.

By the late eighteenth century geology had become popular and respected. More and more scientists began devoting themselves to the study of Earth. From time to time, geologists

An 1860 painting of a geologist performing fieldwork.

would unearth the bones of animals slightly different than animals with which they were familiar. Many found bones that belonged to forms of life unlike any they had ever seen or read about. These discoveries pointed in one direction: the belief in a relatively recent and permanent creation was not in agreement with the physical evidence. Immeasurable species of animal life had undergone significant changes in size and shape. Other species had become extinct. Moreover, this process of change could only have occurred over an incredibly vast number of years.

Geology had a profound influence upon Darwin's life and work. It was after reading Charles Lyell's *Principles of Geology* together with his own geological observations aboard the *Beagle* that the concept of natural selection and thoughts of evolution began taking root in his mind. Not until Darwin had returned to England, however, did his interest in evolution begin developing into an enduring obsession and a workable theory.

A key moment in Darwin's growing belief in the theory of evolution came during a meeting with John Gould, the distinguished British ornithologist who in January 1837 had received the *Beagle*'s bird specimens from the Geological Society of London. In March of that year, Darwin sought out

John Gould *(Courtesy of The Natural History Museum/Alamy)*

71

Gould's opinions on the collection. Gould informed Darwin that his study revealed that the finches of the Galapagos were not different varieties of one species as Darwin had originally believed. Rather, they represented twelve distinct species. Moreover, Darwin thought some of the birds were common wrens and blackbirds, but Gould explained that they were yet another species of finch. Gould also identified three separate species of mockingbirds, each of which Darwin again had assumed were simply different varieties. Gould further noted that the mockingbirds of the Galapagos were related to several other separate species of mockingbirds which resided on the South American mainland.

John Gould made these sketches of finches Darwin discovered at Galapagos.

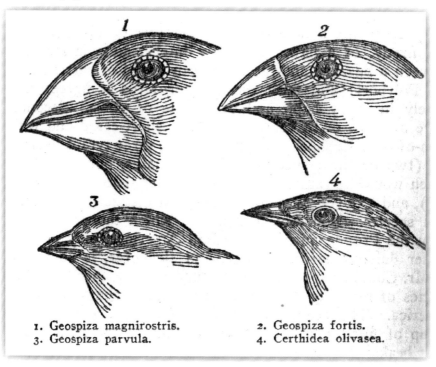

1. Geospiza magnirostris.
3. Geospiza parvula.
2. Geospiza fortis.
4. Certhidea olivasea.

What is a Species?

The term species is one of the most difficult for biologists to satisfactorily define. Darwin himself, in his *Origin of Species*, noted that "no one definition has as yet satisfied all naturalists." And in a letter to his friend, botanist Joseph Hooker, he wrote that to define species is "to define the undefinable."

The eighteenth-century Swedish scholar, Carl Linnaeus, provided the foundation for the modern-day scientific classification of all living things from the broadest category (e.g. animal kingdom) to the most specific category (e.g. *homo sapiens* or humans). Linnaeus based his system upon the taxonomy

Carl Linnaeus, founder of the modern system of plant and animal nomenclature

or structure (morphology) of an organism. Plants and animals which overlapped morphologically were considered members of the same species. Indeed, traditional taxonomic classifications have always been based upon closely related anatomical similarities.

Today biologists tend to avoid identifying species by typology (categories sharing common physical characteristics). Rather, species are identified as populations which can interbreed, which occupy specific niches in nature and which are reproductively isolated from one another by geographical barriers. Thus although certain species may share common physical features, they must be capable of interbreeding and producing fertile offspring to be considered members of the same species.

That the offspring are fertile is of enormous importance when attempting to define species. While at times differing species have been able to successfully reproduce, the products of these unions are almost invariably infertile. A mule is an example of this phenomenon. Mules are the offspring of a male donkey and a female horse. Conversely, a hinny results from the union of a female donkey and a male horse. However, both mules and hinnys are sterile. This is significant from an evolutionary point of view. By being able to successfully interbreed and produce offspring which in turn can also interbreed, a species insures that favorable variations resulting from natural selection remain within the gene pool of that particular species.

Although scientists still encounter occasional difficulty classifying species, a greater comprehension of species exists within the scientific community. The reason for this is the increased understanding of the function of genes in the reproductive process. Indeed, the science of genetics has been able to shed more and more light on the relationships existing both between and among species of all kinds. For example, genetic studies have revealed the differing degrees to which humans are related to each of the nonhuman primates such as chimpanzees, orangutans, gorillas, and others.

The implications of Gould's conclusions prompted Darwin to rethink many of his scientific and religious beliefs. He questioned why an intelligent designer would create so many different species of finches and mockingbirds. The existence of totally different *types* of birds—hawks, robins, owls, sparrows—in a limited geographical area like the Galapagos made sense. What baffled Darwin was the fact that so many different *species* of the same type of bird resided in the same region. As he had done during the voyage of the *Beagle*, Darwin turned to Charles Lyell's *Principles of Geology* for his answer. And as before, one of Lyell's principle arguments kept leaping out at him: the surface and undersurface of the entire Earth is in a state of continual and gradual change. He simply had to carry Lyell's observation one step further to uncover its connection with the birds of the Galapagos.

The finches, like all forms of life, had to adapt to the earth's changes or they would cease to exist. Since the environments on each of the islands differed, the birds evolved over time in different directions depending upon which island they resided. Eventually, the differences among the finches inhabiting each of the islands became so great that they developed into separate species. They looked similar because they all derived from the same ancestral form, a species of finch which most likely originated on the South American mainland.

With that realization, Darwin began to see life as an ongoing process, not a single creative event. All living things were in a constant state of becoming. If it were otherwise and all forms of life remained fixed in structure and function, then life eventually would become extinct. Adaptation would be impossible without the opportunity for change that nature consistently provided. Darwin speculated that far enough back in time a single organism probably existed from which all life originated through an ongoing process of change and adaptation.

In July 1837, Darwin began cataloging data in a confidential notebook which he entitled "Transmutation of Species." For most of the remainder of his life he rarely used the word "evolution," instead choosing terms and phrases like "transmutation," "descent with modification," and "descent theory."

In a diary which he kept to record many of his important thoughts, he made the following entry: "In July opened [my] first book on 'Transmutation of Species' – [I] had been greatly struck from about Month of previous March on [the] character of . . . [bird] species on Galapagos Archipelago. These facts [are the] origin (especially later) of all my views."

The transmutation notebook, the first of six Darwin wrote during the next two years, began with a subtle recognition of his grandfather Erasmus Darwin. As a heading on the first page of the notebook he wrote the word *"Zoonomia,"* a book Erasmus had published forty years earlier. In *Zoonomia,* written as a medical treatise, Erasmus, who believed that all life achieved its present form through a process of evolutionary change, made the unsupported claim that all warm-blooded animals developed from a single, living source. Despite the tribute, it is unlikely that Erasmus had any direct influence upon his grandson's interest in or theory of transmutation.

In the first transmutation notebook, Darwin sought to answer four important questions. What evidence existed for the transmutation of species? What causes species to adapt to an ever-changing environment? What explains the similarities between different species? How do new species develop?

Darwin poured through scientific journals for articles which might shed light on the transmutation phenomenon. He questioned members of the scientific community, both in England and abroad; he always remained cautious when framing his questions so as not to reveal his true intention for asking.

Darwin queried gardeners and horticulturalists attempting to develop different and improved varieties of vegetation by grafting and cross-pollination. He conferred with anyone directly or indirectly involved in the breeding of animals, both domestic (horses, cattle, dogs) and captive (monkeys, lions), and was as concerned with their breeding techniques as he was with the results they achieved. Leaving no avenues unexplored, Darwin even questioned sailors about the migratory habits of birds. He was particularly interested in learning the possible ways birds might relocate from mainland to island or from island to island.

Darwin received most of his information from printed questionnaires which he distributed to anyone familiar with or specifically engaged in animal and plant breeding. One of the questionnaires, an eight-page pamphlet, contained questions like:

> Are physical characteristics acquired in an animal's lifetime passed on to its offspring?

Do certain outstanding features found in individual plants and animals skip a generation before surfacing once again?

Are there instances where the offspring of any union displays unique bodily features found in only one parent rather than features indicating a blending of both parents?

As the notations and sketches in his recorded data indicate, Darwin was now convinced that species do evolve. Yet a large and essential part of the puzzle he had been slowly piecing together remained missing. It was clear to Darwin how physical characteristics such as faster racing horses, fatter cattle, or more intelligent and aggressive watch dogs could be bred by attentive animal breeders. Animals who possessed desirable traits would be isolated by breeders and then crossbred with similar creatures to insure that those traits surface in their offspring. These reproductive techniques would inevitably lead to different varieties of animals and, given enough time, help create new species. The same was true of domesticated plants.

But such was not the case with life in the state of nature where there were no breeding agents available to control reproduction. What occurred among wild plants or animals which helped promote different varieties and eventually new species? How does one account for the variations in speed, size, or aggressiveness that animals in the wild possess? Most important of all, why, as the geological record indicated, did some species become extinct while others survived? In other words, how does natural selection work in living things?

For more than a year after he began his transmutation notebooks, Darwin labored unsuccessfully to uncover the answers to these questions. As his frustration continued to

Thomas Robert Malthus's treatise about population helped Darwin formulate his theory of natural selection. *(Courtesy of Mary Evans Picture Library/Alamy)*

grow, one night in September 1838 he came upon the solution. By a fortunate coincidence he was reading a treatise entitled *An Essay on the Principle of Population*, written by Thomas Robert Malthus (1766-1834), an English political economist. Published in 1798, Malthus attempted to explain why the birth rate in humans, when left unrestrained, would have disastrous effects.

The problem, according to Malthus, was that the population of the human race, and virtually all other animals, tends to increase at a geometric rate (2, 4, 8, 16, 32, etc.). In the case of humans, he wrote, populations will double every twenty five years. On the other hand, food resources available to any growing population only increases at an arithmetic rate (1, 2, 3, 4, 5, etc.). When the numerical gap between population and food resources widens to a critical point, large portions of the inhabitants of a region will inevitably die off having been eliminated by disease, warfare, and/or widespread famine.

Malthus's observation was the insight Darwin had been seeking since he began his transmutation study. In his *Autobiography*, Darwin recorded Malthus's unmistakable importance and impact upon his theory:

> . . . fifteen months after I had begun my systematic enquiry, I happened to read for amusement Malthus on *Population*, and being well prepared to appreciate the struggle for existence which everywhere goes on from long-continued observation of the habits of animals and plants, it at once struck me that under these circumstances favourable variations would tend to be preserved, and unfavourable ones to be destroyed. The result of this would be the formation of new species. Here, then, I had at last got a theory by which to work . . .

Using the Malthusian principle, Darwin was able to finally answer his own questions about change and evolution. He called the solution he came up with "natural selection."

Darwin noted that nearly all living things reproduce at a geometric rate, yet despite this universal tendency, the numbers of any given species usually remain fairly stable. He deduced that there must be a struggle for survival which keeps the population of any plant or animal species comparatively constant. In his *Origin of Species*, Darwin turned to one of the slowest breeding animals, the elephant, to illustrate this point. If one pair of elephants had only six offspring, and if all succeeding offspring of the original six continued to breed at the same rate, in only 750 years the descendants of the first elephants would number 19 million elephants; if elephants survived at the same rate at which they reproduced, the world soon would be overrun with elephants. Therefore, there must be a struggle for survival which keeps the numbers of elephants steady.

In his attempt to determine who survives and who does not, Darwin moved onto another observation: all living things vary. These variations exist both among members of individual species and between members of separate species. From this fact of life, he arrived at a second deduction. Those that survive in the struggle for existence are those with the most favorable variations—those which are naturally best equipped for survival.

In *The Origin of Species*, Darwin presented a concise summary of natural selection:

> As more individuals are produced than can possibly survive, there must in every case be a struggle for existence, either one individual with another of the same species, or with the individuals of distinct species, or with the physical conditions of life. . . . Can it, then, be thought improbable, seeing that variations useful to man have undoubtedly occurred, that other variations useful in some way to each being in the great and complex battle of life, should occur in the course of many successive generations? If such do occur, can we doubt (remembering that many more individuals are born than can possibly survive) that individuals having any advantage, however slight, over others, would have the best chance of surviving and of procreating their kind? On the other hand, we may feel sure that any variation in the least degree injurious would be rigidly destroyed. This preservation

of favourable variations and the rejection of injurious variations,
I call Natural Selection, or the Survival of the Fittest.

Thomas H. Huxley, one of Darwin's earliest and most vocal supporters, remarked when he first learned of the concept of natural selection: "How extremely stupid not to have thought of that [before]!" Huxley's comment was prompted by the fact that Darwin's theory, while revolutionizing the science of biology, was quite straightforward. Huxley was also in effect commenting upon Darwin's greatest strength as a scientist. More so than many notable scientists, Charles Darwin possessed the ability to observe, synthesize, and, most importantly, gather all of his information and resources and create a well-reasoned and credible theory.

Creationism: Belief in a Young Earth and a Permanent Creation

In 1650 James Ussher, an Irish archbishop and scholar, set out to determine the exact year God created the earth. He decided that he could do this by totaling the number of years each of the principal figures of the Old Testament lived as recorded in the Bible. Beginning with Christ (whom historians believed was born in 4 BCE) and working backward to Adam (the first man according to the Bible), he was convinced that he could pinpoint the exact year of creation. After a series of careful calculations, the archbishop arrived at 4004 BCE. In Ussher's day, that would have made the earth about 5,650 years old.

Archbishop Ussher's year of creation was widely

accepted throughout Europe by scientists and theologians alike. Even those who rejected it did not veer far from his date. In the seventeenth century, few educated people believed the age of the earth to be much more than 6,000 years.

Most scientists and theologians also believed that the earth and everything inhabiting it were put there by God as explained in Genesis, the first book of the Bible. More importantly, they held that all of creation was permanent. Since that first moment when God called the earth and its creatures into existence, all living things were created changeless and would remain so until the end of time. Individual plants, animals, and humans would die. But their future generations would continue unaltered.

According to the noted seventeenth-century naturalist and pastor John Ray, it was generally believed "among Divines and Philosophers that since the first creation there have been no species of animals or vegetables lost, no new ones produced." Even Thomas Jefferson, one of America's greatest thinkers wrote in 1782 that "such is the economy of nature that no instance can be produced of [nature] having permitted any one race of her animals to become extinct; of [nature] having found any link in her great work so weak as to be broken."

Since the book of Genesis in the Old Testament revealed a six-day creation, and since the Bible never mentioned that God created anything of significance after Genesis, it could only be concluded that men like Ussher, Ray, and Jefferson were correct. Based upon biblical revelations therefore, the belief in a young earth and a permanent, unchanging creation was held by religious fundamentalists before, during and after Darwin's lifetime.

seven

A Cautious Scientist

I n June 1839, after nearly two years of work, Darwin completed the last of his six transmutation notebooks. He had formulated the basics of his theory of natural selection. Realizing the significance of his work, he continued researching the subject and making inquiries of scientists and other persons familiar with the issue and related areas of study. It was not until May 1842 that he finally decided to write a summary of his thoughts on the mutability of species. Thirty-five pages in length, he expanded the summary two years later into a 189-page manuscript. However he never published or paraded either the abstract or the lengthier version before the scientific community.

Some have argued that for an extensive period of time, Darwin had no intention of publishing his work while he was still alive. A combination of fear of personal denunciation and ridicule as well as the shame it would bring his family, especially Emma, are offered as motivating factors. Yet Darwin's actions indicate that he had no intention of laying his theory to rest during his lifetime. His research on the subject of transmutation continued with increasing enthusiasm.

The most likely reason Darwin was hesitant to go public with his work was the controversial nature of his theory. Darwin feared the scrutiny and negative consequences which might follow publication. He wanted additional proof of his ideas and he felt more time and research would provide him with the evidence he needed. Despite the study and analyses he had already invested in the matter, he still felt vulnerable.

Darwin had good reason to feel at risk. His theory of species origins was in fundamental disagreement with the overwhelming majority of scientific and religious beliefs of the nineteenth century. Even his friend, colleague, and mentor Charles Lyell, whose hypothesis of an ever-changing Earth was at the very center of Darwin's theory, did not accept the premise that living things could change over time. Darwin felt sure that his fellow scientists would not only reject his ideas if he published them prematurely but also think poorly of him personally for doing so. He was convinced that his growing stature as a scientist and his standing in England's scientific community would be placed in serious jeopardy.

Darwin was reminded of the need for caution by an incident which occurred shortly after he had finished his 189-page transmutation manuscript in 1844. In October of that year, Robert Chambers, an author of popular books and magazine articles, anonymously published a work called *Vestiges of the Natural History of Creation*. The book was one of the broadest and most daring statements on evolution published. It was based upon a rigid principle of progressive development, which stated that over many generations, all living things eventually give way to or evolve into a higher type of species. Chambers did argue that the hand of God forged the evolutionary process he was espousing. But God, he claimed, only served as the primary architect who then withdrew from His creation leaving it to develop without interference from Him or any other source.

There were many problems with *Vestiges*, not the least of which was that Chambers was not a trained scientist. The *Vestiges* lacked convincing empirical data to support its arguments. As a result, most of the reviews of the book were brutal. One reviewer compared the author to a prostitute. The respected *British Quarterly* called the book heretical while other journals categorized it as a pseudoscience much like alchemy and astrology. *Vestiges* did however rouse public and scientific opinion on the subject of evolution. And despite the overwhelmingly hostile reviews, it enjoyed enormous sales and went through four editions in its first seven months of publication.

The reception received by *Vestiges* made it clear to Darwin that the atmosphere in England was thick with anti-evolutionary sentiment. Such being the case, he knew that despite his growing fame, his reputation as a meticulous researcher, and his many well-placed friends, popular opinion would not look kindly upon his ideas.

There was another issue that was of great concern to Darwin: his physical condition. At about the time that he had begun work on his transmutation theory, his general health started to decline. He suffered from vomiting, abdominal

This 1830 cartoon ridiculed the idea of evolution almost thirty years before Darwin published *Origin of the Species. (Courtesy of Getty Images)*

pains, chronic flatulence, eczema, generalized rashes, boils, heart palpations, chest pains, body weakness, body swellings, excruciating headaches, depression, anxiety, panic attacks, insomnia, tinnitus, excessive urination, gout, dizziness, and more. The symptoms would pass with time, but his infirmities were often so debilitating that he tired easily and was forced to limit all daily activities. At several periods in his life,

211. Charles Robert Darwin.

der Lithographie von J. H. Mason (1849).

Darwin in 1849 *(Courtesy of Mary Evans Picture Library/Alamy)*

Darwin's health worsened to the point where he was unable to work for months at a time.

No doctors, including his father, were able to successfully diagnosis or treat Darwin's health problems. At various times in his life, treatments like hydrotherapy, bismuth (a metallic element chemically like arsenic and used for gastrointestinal disorders), and laudanum (an opiate tincture which relieves pain) did provide him temporary relief. Yet despite the best efforts of his physicians, there were no permanent or long-standing cures.

In spite of poor health, Darwin continued writing and gathering information on both new and ongoing projects. In addition to publishing *The Voyage of the Beagle* and researching for his notebooks on transmutation, he completed a major work on coral reefs, *The Structure and Distribution of Coral Reefs*, published in May 1842. It took several years to write, and it remains one of the most comprehensive and universally accepted explanations of the creation of coral atolls (a coral island consisting of a lagoon and a surrounding reef).

In the book, Darwin fully explains how a coral atoll is formed over tens of thousands of years. When an extinct volcanic island sinks slowly beneath the sea, the ocean floor surrounding the island sometimes rises in combination with the disappearance of the island. This rising structure becomes the reef which eventually settles just below the water's surface in a saucerlike configuration surrounding the sinking island. In the end, a lagoon will gradually emerge within the inner border of the growing reef. A highly technical work, *The Structure and Distribution of Coral Reefs* was praised upon its release.

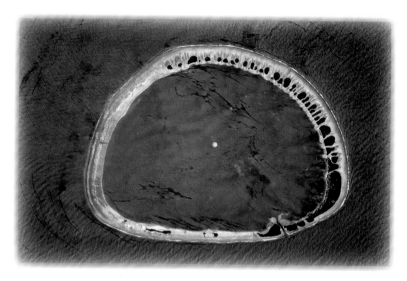

An atoll in the Pacific Ocean. *(Courtesy of the Image Science & Analysis Laboratory, NASA Johnson Space Center)*

Though Darwin embraced and appreciated all of the scientific advantages London offered him—the organizations, resources, and association with other scientists—he never lost his passion for country living. Emma valued the concerts and cultural activities the city provided, but like Charles she was always partial toward rural England. Only one year after moving into Macaw Cottage in London, the couple began looking for a home outside the city.

Other factors also influenced them to move. The noise, crowds, and pollution of the capital city never really suited the quiet, reserved couple. Also, the Darwins did not view London as a place to raise a family (their first son William had been born a year after they were married, and their second child Anne came a year later). Finally, Darwin developed an almost compulsive need for privacy, especially as he began thinking more and more about his new transmutation theory.

Their search for a new home led them to the village of Downe, just sixteen miles southeast of London. Downe, in the county of Kent, was an ideal spot for the Darwins to relocate. It had a population of only five hundred and was quiet and rural, but the village was only a two-hour carriage ride to London, so they'd be able to stay connected to their lives and acquaintances in the city. The Darwins found a house located on the outer edge of the village. Darwin wrote that he was "pleased with the extreme quietness and rusticity of the place." Equally important, the house was perfect in size, the location private, and the 2,200 pounds sale price was a bargain. Darwin's father agreed with the couple's decision to leave London and decided to purchase the house for them.

On September 14, 1842, Darwin, Emma, and their two children moved into their new home, a former parsonage called Down House. Emma was nearly nine months pregnant with their third child. On September 23, Emma gave birth to Mary Eleanor, a small and frail infant who survived only three weeks. However a year later, Henrietta Emma was born. She was followed over the next thirteen years by five brothers (George Howard, Francis, Leonard, Horace, and Charles Waring) and one sister (Elizabeth).

Like many older country homes, Down House was in need of alterations when the Darwins moved in. The bedrooms, while spacious, did not admit adequate light. The Darwins replaced the existing windows with three-paneled bow windows. A large bow window was also installed in the drawing room where Darwin and Emma spent much time together relaxing, reading, and writing letters. As their family grew, another bedroom and a schoolroom were added for use by the children and their governess. Darwin's study, over three

A contemporary view of Down House *(Courtesy of Rolf Richardson/Alamy)*

hundred square feet, was sufficient to accommodate files, chairs, and a desk, and contained enough shelving for his books and collection of letters. Two sizeable windows let in large amounts of sunshine, making it ideal for writing, occasional dissecting, and work with his microscope. Later, as his library and correspondence grew, Darwin was forced to enlarge the study. Emma remodeled the kitchen and pantry to suit her own tastes.

Darwin had many modifications made to the grounds and outside of Down House to satisfy his own need for seclusion. Although the residence lay on the periphery of the village, he still felt it wasn't private enough. A country lane ran past his home making it visible to all passersby. Since the path was within the village's domain, Darwin received permission to excavate one hundred seventy yards of the thoroughfare, lowering it by up to two feet in certain spots. He constructed a wall more than six feet high which ran from one end of the house to the northern end of the property. As a further precaution, he had a mirror installed outside his study so no uninvited persons could catch him unaware. Finally, Darwin constructed the Sandwalk, a gravel path which meandered through a large cluster of trees, assuring him complete privacy.

In his comfortable home, Charles Darwin lived by routine. His son Francis, who studied medicine at Cambridge but instead turned to science, especially botany, worked for

Darwin's Sandwalk on the grounds of his Down House estate.

many years as his father's assistant. In his autobiographical *Reminiscences*, Francis describes his father's typical day:

> He rose early, and took a short turn before breakfast, a habit which began when he went for the first time to a water-cure establishment, and was preserved till almost the end of his life. After breakfasting alone at about 7.45, he went to work at once, considering the 1½ hours between 8 and 9.30 one of his best working times. At 9.30 he came into the drawing-room for his letters – rejoicing if the post was a light one and being sometimes much worried if it was not. He would then hear any family letters read aloud [by Emma] as he lay on the sofa.

After an hour in the drawing-room, Darwin would return to his study where he continued research until noon. Regardless of the weather, he then would go outdoors and walk for one hour through the Sandwalk, sometimes going into the green-house to monitor his plant experiments. After lunch, Darwin relaxed on the sofa in his drawing room and read the daily newspaper. From two to three he wrote letters while sitting in the oversized chair in his study. Following an hour's rest in his bedroom where Emma would read a novel to him, he would take an afternoon stroll.

The rest of the day followed a similar pattern: working in his study, relaxing in the drawing room, a turn on the Sandwalk, a light dinner with the family, a backgammon game with Emma, more reading in the drawing room, and a piano concert by Emma. By ten o'clock each night, Charles would enter his bedroom, change into his bed clothes, and be ready for sleep no later than 10:30. The only times he would deviate from this daily routine were those periods when he was too ill or felt too weak to leave his bedroom in the morning.

During their first years at Down House, the Darwins only occasionally ventured beyond the borders of Kent. Most often, it was to visit family in Shrewsbury or Maer. At times, they traveled to a health facility either for Darwin or if one of the children was ill. Occasionally, Darwin went to London to do research, visit his brother Erasmus, or attend meetings at various scientific societies. Whenever possible, however, he avoided trips to the city. If any specimens or documents were waiting there for him, he would send his butler Joseph Parslow to pick them up. Parslow, who one of Darwin's aunts described as being singularly devoted, also traveled about collecting materials from horticulturalists and animal breeders with whom Darwin was corresponding.

As the years passed, Darwin's already infrequent trips away from his estate grew rarer still. He wrote: "Few persons can have lived a more retired life than we [Charles and Emma] have done. Besides short visits to the houses of relations, and occasionally to the seaside or elsewhere, we have gone nowhere."

Though Darwin's cloistered lifestyle and tendency toward panic disorders have led some to believe he may have been agoraphobic (a person who rarely, if ever, leaves the confines of his or her own home in order to avoid large gatherings or public places), or socially hindered in some other way, it seems unlikely. Darwin, although reserved in temperament, was not painfully shy or pathologically reclusive. He was always composed and gracious in the company of others. Neither was he unappreciative of, nor unable to cope with, his mounting fame. Throughout his entire life Darwin never hesitated at expressing the pleasure and fulfillment he experienced from the sales of his books and the admiration of his peers.

Darwin was extraordinarily vigilant, with a strong need for privacy. Darwin needed someone in his life to help soften his caution. Ideally, that person would be a learned confidant with whom he could fully and comfortably disclose his ideas, and who saw both the logic and potential of his theory. While he and Emma shared a deep attachment, she was not a scientist and was overly emotional when it came to his work. His dependable old friend Reverend John Henslow did not—and would not ever—accept Darwin's belief that not only do plants and animals evolve, they do so at the blind whim of nature. His colleague Charles Lyell, while always encouraging, never comfortably embraced the idea that living things could transform into new species over vast periods of time.

Although he did not realize it until the connection was made, Darwin needed a close, likeminded friend whose knowledge and scientific credentials would make him both a trustworthy intimate and a reliable advisor. He found that ally in Joseph Dalton Hooker. Although the two had met in London in 1839, it would be five years before the acquaintanceship strengthened into a bond that helped Darwin at first inch forward and then later race toward the publication of his *Origin of Species*. Many years into their association, Darwin recognized Hooker as the one person from whom he had always received sympathy.

eight

The Origin of Species

J oseph Dalton Hooker was one of the nineteenth-century's leading scientists and probably England's best known botanist. Born in Halesworth, England, on June 30, 1817, he was the second son of Sir William Jackson Hooker, director of the Royal Botanic Gardens at Kew in London. Hooker attended the University of Glasgow where he received an M.D. in 1839. Botany, however, always remained his primary passion. As the son of a widely respected and honored botanist, Joseph spent much of his childhood surrounded by botanical specimens, memorabilia, and specialists. While still a young man, his knowledge and competence in botany was equal to that of many veterans of the science. Shortly after receiving his medical degree, Hooker took the job of assistant surgeon/botanist aboard the HMS *Erebus*. The *Erebus* undertook a three-year governmental expedition to Antarctica under the command of Sir James Ross. Hooker learned much on the voyage, just as Darwin had aboard the *Beagle.*

A prolific writer, when he returned to England in 1843 Hooker began publishing books on the flora of Antarctica, New Zealand, and Australia as well as accounts of his own adventures while aboard the *Erebus.* He was invited as resident botanist on other government-sponsored explorations, including one to Northern India from 1847 to 1851. In 1855 he became assistant director of the Royal Botanic Gardens. Upon the death of his father in 1865, Hooker was promoted to director, a position he held until his retirement in 1885.

Hooker and Darwin met in London in the summer of 1839. A chance meeting, Hooker and a former officer of the *Beagle* were discussing Hooker's upcoming expedition on the *Erebus* when Darwin happened along. Hooker was well aware of Darwin and his work. Through his father William's connections, Hooker had been given the opportunity to read proof sheets of Darwin's *Journal of Researches* before its formal printing. Years later Hooker recalled being so impressed by the quality and scope of the *Journal* that he admitted to sleeping with it under his pillow every night. He claimed he placed the pages there so that they would be available to read in the event he awoke before it was time to rise from bed.

Shortly after Hooker returned from Antarctica in 1843, Darwin offered him the opportunity to study and catalogue the plants Darwin had gathered during the *Beagle*'s stopover in Tierra del Fuego at the southernmost tip of South America. Hooker agreed to the offer, leaving Darwin elated by the young man's enthusiasm and later by his competence in evaluating the collection. Darwin began developing a fondness for Hooker, describing him as "one of my best friends throughout life." He

A romanticized depiction of J. D. Hooker collecting plants in the Himalayas. *(Courtesy of Mary Evans Picture Library/Alamy)*

decided to share with Hooker the full range of his ideas on transmutation. (Earlier, Darwin had discussed his theory—although not in great depth—with Charles Lyell and Reverend Leonard Jenyns, a vicar from Cambridge and an expert naturalist. He received a cool reception from both.)

In a letter dated January 11, 1844, Darwin first began sharing his ideas about the evolution of species with Hooker. In the final paragraph of the letter, Darwin wrote of his conviction that species do mutate:

> Besides a general interest about the Southern lands, I have been now ever since my return [from the *Beagle's* voyage] engaged in a very presumptuous work and which I know no one individual who would not say a very foolish one. I was so struck with [the] distribution of Galapagos organisms. . . . and with the character of the American fossil mammifers [mammals]. . . . that I determined to collect blindly every sort of fact, which could bear [in] any way on what are species. I have read heaps of agricultural and horticultural books, and have never ceased collecting facts – At last gleams of light have come, and I am almost convinced (quite contrary to [the] opinion I started with) that species are not (it is like confessing a murder) immutable. . . . I think I have found out (here's presumption!) the simple way by which species become exquisitely adapted to various ends.

Much to Darwin's delight—if not surprise—Hooker was excited over his theory even though he was not in complete agreement with it. From his own botanical work, Hooker came to realize that plant species can and do change over many generations. He was unsure, though, of the extensiveness of the change. He was not convinced one species could evolve into another. It would be at least ten years before Hooker came to fully accept Darwin's concept of evolution by natural selection.

Still, Hooker had responded positively to Darwin's theories, and he quickly became an indispensable friend. In January 1847, Darwin asked him to read the transmutation manuscript he had written nearly three years earlier; Hooker's remarks proved thoughtful, incisive, and invaluable. He was direct and persuasive with his negative and positive comments, both of which Darwin accepted with eagerness. Later, as friendship flourished, Hooker became a regular visitor at the Darwin home. Emma was pleased with Charles's new and close colleague, and always went out of her way to make Hooker feel welcome. Hooker's role as a friend and advisor had become so beneficial that when Hooker left for his three-year visit to India, Darwin was visibly upset over the vacuum it left in his life.

By the mid-1840s, Darwin's standing as a scientist was derived almost entirely from his impressive list of publications in the field of geology. In addition to his *Journal of Researches* (1839) which Darwin revised in 1845, his published works included: *The Structure and Distribution of Coral Reefs* (1842), *Geological Observations on Volcanic Islands* (1844), and *Geological Observations on South America* (1846). Yet if Darwin was to have any credibility when the time came to publicize his theory of evolution, it was essential that he establish a reputation as a biologist/naturalist. Hooker kept pressing this fact home to Darwin, who, while aware of it himself, had taken no action. Hoping to fill the significant gap that existed in his credentials as a naturalist, Darwin turned to the barnacle.

Darwin had developed an interest in barnacles during his explorations off the coast of Chile in 1835 and spoke sincerely of committing himself one day to a serious examination of

Darwin's eight-year examination of barnacles made him a scientist of international renown and also provided insight into how species change.

them. Moreover since his work on transmutation began after his interest in barnacles, a study of the marine crustacean would add additional substance to his growing body of information on species formation. Most importantly, relevant and accurate information on barnacles was woefully lacking. A reliable research paper of the depth and quality Darwin was capable of achieving would surely be well-received.

Darwin began his study of barnacles as he had most of his previous works, by requesting specimens and information from friends and specialists throughout the world. In a letter to Syms Covington dated March 30, 1849, he asked for samples of sea rocks, shells, or corals brought ashore by gales and the tide.

Covington, a shipmate aboard the *Beagle* who Darwin later took on as a servant, was specifically instructed (as were all correspondents) to mail the specimens in the same condition in which they were found. Darwin stressed the need to forward samples in an unspoiled state since he then would have the opportunity to determine if parasites or any other sea creatures attached to the barnacles were involved in the crustacean's life and reproductive cycle. He reminded Covington "that barnacles are conical little shells, with a sort of four-valved lid on the top. There are others with long flexible footstalk, fixed to floating objects, and sometimes cast on shore."

Darwin's work with barnacles lasted nearly eight years. For two of those years, extensive bouts of vomiting made it nearly impossible for him to make any significant progress. Yet despite his chronic illness and the death of his beloved daughter Annie in 1851, Darwin persevered. His persistence yielded impressive results which included four comprehensive monographs on cirripedia, the subclass under which biologists classify barnacles: *A Monograph of the Sub-class Cirripedia* (1851), *A Monograph of the Fossil Pedunculated Cirripeds of Great Britain* (1851), *A Monograph of the Sessile Cirripeds* (1854), and *A Monograph of the Fossil Sesile Cirripeds* (1854). In November 1853, the year before Darwin published the final barnacle monograph, the Royal Society honored him with the Royal Medal for his geological publications drawn from the voyage of the *Beagle* and for his ongoing studies with barnacles.

With the publication of his cirripedia studies, Charles Darwin truly became a scientist of international standing. His monographs were touted—and still are—as the definitive study on the subject of barnacles. Those eight years spent studying the barnacle also presented him with an invaluable new insight into his primary interest, the origin of species.

If all living things derived from one primordial, unisexual life form—as Darwin believed was a real possibility—then where and how did the separation of the sexes take place? The barnacle provided him with a possible answer. Darwin discovered that his barnacles were hermaphroditic, that is organisms having both male and female reproductive parts. From this fact he arrived at the plausible conclusion that the origin of separate sexes most likely derived from a divergence or split that occurred eons ago in a hermaphroditic life form similar to the barnacle. That would then explain the genesis of true sexual reproduction, which, in turn, provided the foundation for the more rapid origin and spread of variations within species.

Although professionally rewarding, the barnacle research and publications took much longer than Darwin had anticipated. By the autumn of 1854, he wrote Hooker that he was eager to once again start thinking about his work on transmutation. This time the caution and fear that he had felt when faced with sharing his work on evolution were considerably diminished. The cirripedia studies had given him credibility in the field of biology, and though he would likely still be challenged if he publicized his ideas, at least he would not immediately be dismissed as irresponsible and contemptible.

There was another reason why Darwin felt more comfortable pressing ahead with his work on transmutation. The 1850s in England and elsewhere witnessed the beginning of a liberal revolution in thinking that was opening the door to new and even radical ideas. One prominent philosopher in particular, Herbert Spencer, began overtly advocating the

By the 1850s, a more liberal climate in England allowed Herbert Spencer, a prominent philosopher, to openly advocate a belief in evolution without risking public outrage.

belief in organic evolution. In a widely read article entitled "The Development Hypothesis" published in 1852 in the acclaimed British periodical *Leader*, Spencer implied that there was broad agreement among scientists that the number of living and extinct plant and animal species number in excess of 10 million. He then wrote:

Well, which is the most rational theory about these ten millions of species? Is it most likely that there have been ten millions of special creations? Or is it most likely that by continual modifications, due to change of circumstances, ten millions of varieties may have been produced, as varieties are being produced still? . . . Even could the supporters of the development hypothesis merely show that the production of species by the process of modification is conceivable, they would be in a better position than their opponents.

While he now was far more at ease writing on the issue of evolution, Darwin's predisposition for detailed research continued. Despite the frequent prodding of his friends Hooker and Lyell that he commit his ideas to writing and publish as soon as possible, Darwin was adamant that he investigate the subject further.

Darwin believed that the more evidence he put forth to bolster his theory of natural selection, the fewer dismissals he would receive. Although he was correct in that assumption, it prevented him from fully appreciating the reasons that his colleagues insisted that he move quickly toward publication. Far more than fear of public rejection, Hooker and Lyell worried that a theory of evolution similar to Darwin's might be developed by another scientist working independent of their friend. If Darwin was beaten to publication, the credit Darwin deserved for his decades of researching and amassing physical evidence would all be lost.

Because of the more liberal temper of the times, the subject of evolution was increasingly finding its way into many public and scientific discussions and journals. Herbert Spencer's article in the *Leader* was but one example. The widely known theory of acquired characteristics put forth by the Frenchman Jean-Baptiste Lamarck (1744-1829), although discussed for nearly three-quarters of a century, was broadening its base of advocates (Spencer being one of them).

Of far greater concern was Alfred Russel Wallace. Wallace, fourteen years younger than Darwin, was a naturalist working in Malaysia, where he had begun gathering evidence supporting his belief in the formation of new species. In 1855, he published his views in an article in the *Annals and Magazine of Natural History*. Entitled "On the Law Which Has Regulated the Introduction of New Species," the author unveiled a theory which was uncomfortably close to Darwin's. In fact, having heard of Darwin's interest and

Jean-Baptiste Lamarck (*Courtesy of The London Art Archive/Alamy*)

Jean-Baptiste Lamarck and the Theory of Acquired Characteristics

Jean-Baptiste Lamarck, a Frenchman, was one of the first modern scientists to propose that plants and animals evolve by natural means. He was born in 1744, the youngest of eleven children of an old but impoverished family of aristocrats. Although his father insisted that he become a Catholic priest, Lamarck eventually gravitated toward his true passion, the biological sciences. The field in which he chose to specialize was botany.

Lamarck's contribution to the subject of evolution was his theory of "acquired characteristics." To Lamarck, the environment in which a plant or animal exists provides the answer to why and how evolutionary change occurs in each animal. Animals living in a cold climate where the food supply is limited will differ in size, shape, agility, and numerous other characteristics from animals residing in a warm, lush environment. These differences result from the demands environmental factors place upon an animal's physical makeup. For example, a mountain goat will exhibit greater nimbleness of foot and a leaner, more muscular body than will a lumbering cow whose habitat is a flat, lush green valley and whose food resources are abundant and provided by the dairy farmer.

It appears obvious that the geographical location and circumstances under which an organism lives forces that organism, if it is to survive, to use certain parts of its body more frequently than others. Accordingly, Lamarck concluded that "the more frequent and sustained use of any organ [or body part] strengthens, develops and enlarges that organ, and gives it a power commensurate with the duration of this employment of it." Lamarck then drew this conclusion: the changes that take place in a body part or organ are subsequently passed on to the offspring of that organism. In other words, characteristics acquired during an organism's lifetime are transmitted to its offspring and, after a sufficient period of time and assuming acquired changes continue to occur, eventually a new species will result.

Lamarck's doctrine of use or disuse is based upon this idea. By not using a particular bodily part or organ, that part or organ will gradually atrophy and in time may even disappear. Larmarck stated unequivocally that the "permanent disuse of an organ as a consequence of acquired habits gradually impoverishes it, and in the end causes it to disappear, or even annihilates it altogether." He even speculated that if two children (a boy and a girl) had their left eyes permanently covered from the moment of birth and then interbred as adults and if that same procedure was repeated over numerous generations with the offspring of the original pair, it would affect vision in the left eye. Eventually the ancestors of the original couple would lose the use of their left eye and, in time, the eye would disappear entirely. Their right eyes would probably move toward the center to compensate for loss of the left one and help to restore a wider field of vision.

Lamarck's theory of acquired characteristics was the dominant evolutionary theory until the twentieth century. The science of genetics helped disprove the idea that features acquired in an organism's lifetime can be passed on to its offspring. Geneticists have shown that genetic changes on the cellular level alone can give rise to inheritable changes in an organism's phenotype (physical characteristics). In fact, the only beneficiary of a muscular body will be the individual who developed it through physical exercise and not the progeny of that individual. (Recent "Neo-Lamarckian" studies however have shown that certain genes actually may shift or "jump" in order to help adjust an organism to changes in its environment. Since the change is genetic in nature, that characteristic can be passed on to the next generation.)

This 1863 woodcarving depicts Alfred Russel Wallace and fellow naturalist Henry Walter Bates collecting specimens from the Amazon in 1848. *(Courtesy of The Print Collector/Alamy)*

work in the area of species development, Wallace forwarded a copy of his *Annals* article to Darwin, hoping to solicit the elder scientist's learned opinion. Darwin responded positively to Wallace's work, and although he recognized some areas in which Wallace's study paralleled his own, he still saw no need to hastily move forward.

On May 14, 1856, Darwin finally began writing his work on his theory of species transmutation. He gave the new book the working title *Natural Selection.* More than twenty-five years worth of thinking, experimentation, collecting specimens, notebooks, letters to and from friends and colleagues, monographs, and solicitations from fellow scientists were all used to support his central thesis: all living things, whether plants or animals, evolve. Furthermore, evolution is not guided by a supreme power. Within a half year, he had completed two chapters which dealt with variations among domesticated plants and animals. Early in 1857, he had finished the chapters dealing with the variations species exhibit in nature. He then began describing the relationship between the subject of variation and the principle he had derived from Thomas Malthus, namely that there is a struggle for existence where those who are most fit generally will be the survivors.

The demands of research and extensive writing began to take a toll on his health. Added to the stress of his work, on December 6, 1856, his sixth son Charles Waring was born, and it soon became clear that the boy was mentally challenged. In April 1857, as he had in the past during periods of extreme pressure, Darwin went for hydropathic therapy at Dr. Edward Lane's clinic in Farnham, about thirty miles west of his home. He returned home after two weeks at the spa only to suffer a relapse little more than a month later. After another two weeks of water therapy in June, he returned home to continue working.

The next twelve months passed similarly: Darwin energetically labored on his book for extended periods of time, then grew exhausted and ill and forced to spend several days recuperating in bed or seeking therapy at Dr. Lane's Clinic. Adding to his stress was the realization that *Natural Selection* was proving a far weightier project than originally anticipated. Most likely it would culminate as a multivolume project surpassing a half million words in length. However by June 1858, Darwin began sensing his work was nearing completion.

Then quite unexpectedly, on June 18, 1858, Darwin received a large envelope from Alfred Russel Wallace. The package contained a letter and an essay written by Wallace entitled "On the Tendency of Varieties to Depart Indefinitely from the Original Type." In the letter, Wallace asked Darwin's opinion of the essay and further requested that Darwin send it to his colleague and friend Charles Lyell for his assessment.

Upon reading Wallace's work, Darwin was shocked. The essay was an attempt to explain why species vary, and it did so in terms nearly identical to Darwin's own concept of natural selection. That same day, Darwin wrote Lyell expressing his stunned disbelief. Forwarding Wallace's paper to the geologist he wrote:

> He (Wallace) has to day sent me the enclosed & asked me to forward it to you. . . .Your words have come true with a vengeance that I should be forestalled. You said this when I explained to you here (at Down House) very briefly my views of "Natural Selection" depending on the Struggle for existence. – I never saw a more striking coincidence. If Wallace had my sketch written out in 1842 he could not have made a better short abstract! Even his terms now stand as Heads of my Chapters. Please return me the [manuscript] which he does not say he wishes me to publish; but I shall of course at once write & offer to send to any Journal. So all my originality, whatever it may amount to, will be smashed.

A week later, Darwin again contacted Lyell. In the second letter, he explained that since he was now aware of Wallace's latest work and theory, it would be dishonorable for him to move forward as though he were unmindful of the facts. Making what had to have been one of the most painful decisions of his life, Darwin explained to Lyell:

> There is nothing in Wallace's sketch which is not written out much fuller in my sketch copied in 1844, and read by Hooker some dozen years ago. About a year ago I sent a short sketch

of which I have [a] copy of my views . . . to Asa Gray [the most influential American botanist of the nineteenth century], so that I could most truly say & prove that I take nothing from Wallace. I should be *extremely* glad now to publish a sketch of my general views in about a dozen pages or so. But I cannot persuade myself that I can do so honourably. Wallace says nothing about publication, & I enclose his letter. – But as I had not intended to publish any sketch, can I do so honourably because Wallace has sent me an outline of his doctrine? – I would far rather burn my whole book than that he or any man should think that I had behaved in a paltry spirit.

Charles Lyell immediately notified Joseph Hooker of Darwin's dilemma. Both men, as friends of Darwin and scientists themselves, were disturbed. There was never any question in anyone's mind that Wallace had arrived at his conclusions independent of Darwin. Nonetheless, it was obvious that in terms of the massive amount of research he had expended and his priority in time, Darwin deserved credit for the theory of evolution by natural selection. After deliberating, Lyell and Hooker arrived at a solution which would not violate Darwin's principles nor could be construed as treating Wallace unfairly.

On July 1, 1858, The Linnean Society, the world's oldest biological organization, had scheduled a meeting at its headquarters in London. Lyell and Hooker convinced Thomas Bell, the president of the society, to have papers on natural selection by Darwin and Wallace offered at that meeting to the membership. Lyell and Hooker then specifically arranged for the presentation of an outline of Darwin's 1844 manuscript to be read along with the letter he wrote a year earlier to Asa Gray explaining his theory. Wallace's 1858 essay was to follow the Darwin readings. Finally, it would be explained to the membership that both men arrived at their conclusions independently and that Darwin had been working on his theory for more than twenty years.

Alfred Russel Wallace agreed to the presentation. He acknowledged Darwin's right to claim priority of the theory of natural selection. Furthermore, he stated that his most recent essay was overwhelmed by the massive amount of work Darwin had done over the years. (Indeed, in 1889, when Wallace published his own book about evolution by natural selection, he entitled it *Darwinism*.) As for Darwin, he at first worried that Wallace would reject the arrangement made with Thomas Bell, but upon learning of Wallace's reaction and afterward becoming personally acquainted with him, Darwin praised Wallace for his generosity and fairness. The two scientists soon developed an abiding friendship.

When the reading of the theories on natural selection occurred, contrary to what Darwin had expected, the Linnean group reacted with quiet detachment. With what would later prove to be one of the greatest understatements in the history of science, Thomas Bell noted that the Society's meetings in 1858 had "not, indeed, been marked by any of those striking discoveries which at once revolutionize, so to speak, the department of science on which they bear."

What Is Evolution?

The theory of evolution teaches that all living things, both plants and animals, have originated from preexisting types through a process of genetic change. Moreover, evolutionary theory assumes that all life can ultimately be traced to a simple, self-replicating organic form which existed more than 2 billion years ago. Reduced to its simplest meaning, evolution may therefore be defined as any change in hereditary endowment over time.

More than 10 million (perhaps as many as 30 million) different species of plants and animals have evolved during this 2-billion year period. Each new species of life form has come about through a process of change and adaptation. When change occurs, if the change is advantageous and offers its recipient survival advantages, the organism experiencing the change will be better suited to adapt to its environment. While several explanations for the causes of evolutionary change have been offered by scientists, historically the two most widely accepted have been the theories of natural selection (associated with Charles Darwin) and acquired characteristics, also known as the doctrine of "use and disuse" (associated with Jean-Baptiste Lamarck).

Today, modern biology is grounded in Darwin's concept of evolution by natural selection. Indeed, it is natural selection which, in effect, unites the amoeba and the Nobel laureate. Since all life derives from the same source and is subject to the same laws of nature for its evolutionary development, all living things are by nature connected.

Biologists argue that abundant evidence exists as proof of the evolution of species. One such example is the presence of vestigial parts or organs in many animals. A vestigial body part is a structure present in any animal

The wings of flightless birds like ostriches are considered vestigial parts, and biologists argue that such features are proof that species evolve over time.

which has lost its original function and, in many cases, serves no function at all. However, its very existence is indicative of an earlier period in the evolution of the species during which the part was fully functioning. For example, the dissection of a whale reveals vestigial leg bones in the back of the whale's body. These leg bones point to an ancestral species which resided on land and had full use of its hind legs. A further example would be the wings of flightless birds such as the ostrich and the penguin. The presence of these non-functioning wings is evidence of ancestral species where the wings were fully functioning parts.

Historically, evolution has been at odds with Creationism, a strict, literal interpretation of the biblical account of the origin and development of life. Creationists argue that all life, past, present and future, is the result of a single creative act by a supreme being. Furthermore, creationists believe that all life is immutable—that from the first moment of creation, life in all of its inestimable varied forms has been unchanging. There is, however, a compromise position. Frequently referred to as theistic evolution, it combines biological evolution with divine creation, claiming that all living things have evolved from earlier forms and that God is the first cause and prime mover of the process.

nine

The Aftermath of *Origin*

Despite the Linnean Society's seeming indifference to the readings on natural selection, the theory Darwin had been perfecting and guarding for twenty years from all but a select few was at long last available for public scrutiny. The possibilities now existed that, in addition to Alfred Russel Wallace, any scientist or layman could pick up on the idea and publish an article or book dealing with descent by natural selection. Darwin and his friends realized that delaying publication, for whatever reason, was no longer a feasible option.

After carefully evaluating the different directions he could take, Darwin concluded that the manuscript he had been working on for the past two years was simply too long and involved for his intended audience, the general reading public. On July 20, 1858, he began writing a shorter, more simplified version of *Natural Selection*. From time to time, he sent completed chapters to Hooker and Lyell soliciting their suggestions. Working at a steady rate and all but ignoring his characteristic bouts of illness, Darwin completed the shorter version by April 1859. The final manuscript tallied in at more than 155,000 words—much shorter than its forerunner but substantial nonetheless.

Darwin turned to his friend Charles Lyell for help in getting the book published. Lyell suggested John Murray, the man who had published Lyell's *Principles of Geology*. Although less than enthusiastic, Murray, influenced by Lyell's reputation and insistence, agreed to take on the Darwin manuscript. After several months of preparation, publisher and author settled upon the book's title: *On the Origin of Species by Means of Natural Selection or the Preservation of Favoured Races in the Struggle for Life*. Murray initially planned to print 750 copies of the first edition, but subsequently increased the press run to 1,250 copies as unexpected orders began pouring in.

On November 24, 1859, when the work was released for sale throughout England, the entire printing sold out on that first day. The immediate response to *The Origin of Species* by the scientific community ranged from wholehearted acceptance to fierce opposition.

Joseph Hooker publicly concurred with Darwin's arguments, but the prominent American botanist Asa Gray, a longtime supporter of Darwin and his work, insisted God was the force behind natural selection itself. Charles Lyell, although he agreed with the theory in its essentials, never completely endorsed Darwin's conclusions. Although disappointed, Darwin understood that Lyell's recent association with the English royal family made his situation precarious. From Cambridge, Adam Sedgwick and John Henslow openly

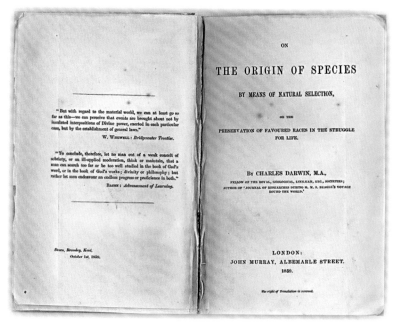

When *The Origin of Species* was released for sale in England in 1859, the entire print-run sold out on the first day.

disagreed with Darwin. Both were clergymen as well as scientists, and could not accept the idea of the existence of life fashioned by anything but a creator God as explained in the Bible.

Louis Agassiz, a well-known Swiss geologist and zoologist who had corresponded with Darwin for many years, dismissed *Origin* as being without scientific foundation. Agassiz, by that time a professor of natural history at Harvard University in the United States, believed that all species were the result of divine creation. Richard Owen attacked the concept of natural selection, arguing that it could not work without a selector— that is all changes occurring in nature require some mechanism (i.e. a selector) which would be responsible for generating each of those changes. Because he did not believe such a mechanism existed, he held that new species had to arise spontaneously. One of England's foremost anatomists, it was Owen who more than twenty years earlier had examined and praised the collection of fossils Darwin had brought back from South America.

Perhaps the fiercest and most vocal of Darwin's detractors was the English zoologist St. George Mivart. Although

Louis Agassiz, a Swiss geologist, was among those who disagreed with Darwin's hypothesis of transmutation.

originally on friendly terms with Darwin, Mivart's negative reaction to *The Origin of Species* drove a wedge between the two scientists. In his book *On the Genesis of Species* (1871), an undisguised attack on Darwin's publication, Mivart took serious issue with the idea of gradualism, the very foundation of natural selection. According to Mivart, the age of the earth is too short to have permitted the gradual evolution of so many and such diverse numbers of species. In *Nature and Thought* (1882) and *The Origin of Human Reason* (1889), he further attacked Darwin for implying that humanity's sense of morality and ethics derived from the same evolutionary path nature provided its animal ancestors. He declared that the human intellect was bestowed upon men and women exclusively by divine providence, not the impersonal forces of nature. In a letter to Wallace, Darwin complained of Mivart's personal attacks and that his book *On the Genesis of Species* was undermining Darwin's arguments favoring natural selection.

One of the most interesting and frequently related episodes connected with the publication of *The Origin of Species* was a debate that took place in June 1860. The British

Thomas Huxley

Association for the Advancement of Science (BAAS) was having its annual meeting at Oxford University. The meeting was to last several days and it was announced that the subject of evolution would be discussed on June 30, 1860, the final day. Thomas Huxley and a prominent Anglican bishop, Samuel Wilberforce, were among those expected to speak that day. Wilberforce, an extremely gifted orator, was strongly opposed to all evolutionary theories. Huxley, who had a growing reputation as "Darwin's Bulldog," was one of the naturalist's most passionate supporters. Over eight hundred attended the debate.

Wilberforce, known as "Soapy Sam" because of his silky and slippery manner of debating, preceded Huxley to the speaker's lectern. Not a trained scientist, Wilberforce relied upon his oratorical skills to help him through the debate. For thirty minutes he hammered away at *The Origin of Species*, attempting to discredit the Darwinian evolutionary theory of

A caricature of Samuel Wilberforce from an 1869 *Vanity Fair*. *(Courtesy of Mary Evans Picture Library/Alamy)*

descent with modification. Finally, he turned to Huxley and asked in a mocking tone whether Huxley traced his descent from a "monkey" on his grandfather or his grandmother's side of the family. When Wilberforce finished his speech, Huxley turned to the speaker sitting next to him on the stage and said: "The Lord hath delivered him into mine hands."

Huxley rose to give his reply, as a quiet spread throughout the audience. He responded with eloquence and logic, repudiating Wilberforce's arguments, which he believed were simply a recycling of Richard Owen's criticism. He reminded the audience that Darwin's idea of natural selection provided the biological sciences with the grand unifying principle it had long lacked. He ended his argument by stating directly to Wilberforce: "If I would rather have a miserable ape for a grandfather or a man highly endowed by nature and possessed of great means and influence, and yet who employs those faculties for the mere purpose of introducing ridicule into a grave scientific discussion—I unhesitatingly affirm my preference for the ape."

Following Huxley's speech, the packed room broke into a

Thomas Huxley, "Darwin's Bulldog"

Thomas Henry Huxley (1825-1895), although a prominent English scientist in his own right, is perhaps best known for his aggressive and effective championing of Charles Darwin and his theory of evolution by natural selection. Born near London the seventh of eight children, his father taught mathematics at the local school. Although Huxley himself only had two years of formal education as a child, he was an insatiable reader, especially in the sciences.

As a boy, he was able to obtain a position as a medical apprentice from which he went on to win a scholarship to the medical school at Charing Cross Hospital, later receiving medals for his work in physiology and organic chemistry. He went on to teach natural history and paleontology at the Government School of Mines in London.

He and Darwin struck up a friendship in 1856 about the time Darwin began writing *The Origin of Species*. At first, Huxley did not agree with Darwin's ideas on natural selection. However once he was won over to the theory, he began devoting much of his intellectual energy to its support. For his efforts he became known as "Darwin's Bulldog."

Huxley's acceptance of Darwinian evolution was not without qualification. He never agreed with Darwin that the process of change and subsequent adaptation experienced by evolving species were gradual. Rather, he came out in favor of a process called saltation. The word derives from the Latin, *saltus*, which is most often translated as "leap." Huxley argued that changes in any species from generation to generation generally occur in leaps or large, measurable increments rather than gradually. Saltation is somewhat similar to a relatively recent theory called punctuated equilibrium. Published in 1972 by paleontologists Niles Eldridge and Stephen Jay Gould, the pair theorized that species experience little or no change over long geological periods of time. This static period of "equilibrium" then ends with a short, "punctuated" interlude of rapid evolutionary change.

Thomas Huxley was a gifted and prolific writer whose prose style was highly praised by countless authors including famed American journalist H. L. Mencken. Huxley's most celebrated book, *Evidence as to Man's Place in Nature* (1863), was one of the first to suggest an ancestral link exists between humans and apes. Huxley was the father of biographer Leonard Huxley and the grandfather of biologist Julian Huxley and fiction author Aldous Huxley.

The frontispiece to Huxley's *Evidence as to Man's Place in Nature*, one of the first books to suggest a link between humans and apes.

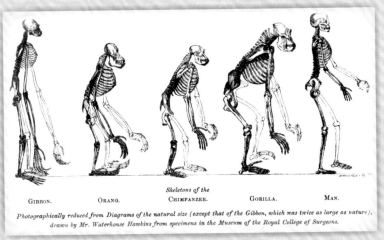

Sheletons of the

GIBBON.   ORANG.   CHIMPANZEE.   GORILLA.   MAN.

Photographically reduced from Diagrams of the natural size (except that of the Gibbon, which was twice as large as nature), drawn by Mr. Waterhouse Hawkins from specimens in the Museum of the Royal College of Surgeons.

frenzy. Reports claimed that Lady Brewster, a prominent aristocrat and regular attendee of BAAS meetings reeled, fainted, and had to be carried out. Robert Fitzroy, the captain of HMS *Beagle* who had since risen to the rank of admiral, was in the audience with a Bible in hand and screamed insults directed at Darwin and Huxley.

While the debate raged about his theory, Darwin was indisposed most of the time. While Huxley was debating Wilberforce a stomach ailment that kept growing worse forced him to seek rest and hydrotherapy for ten days at Dr. Edward Lane's health establishment.

An 1870 engraving of men undergoing hydrotherapy. Darwin often underwent the treatment to relieve his physical ailments. (*Courtesy of Wellcome Library, London. Wellcome Images*)

BATHING.

An important part of the criticism leveled at *The Origin of Species* was grounded in what the book implied rather than what was actually written. Many, such as Bishop Wilberforce, took grave issue with what they believed was a thinly veiled inference by Darwin that a connection existed between humans and apes. To acknowledge that most living things could evolve into different species given a complex interplay of time, the environment, and some sort of mechanism inherent in virtually all life-forms was something which many could accept. But to suggest that humans and apes shared a common ancestry denied humans their special part of creation, separated from the rest by God.

Darwin carefully avoided including all mention of human origins in the first edition of *The Origin of Species.* It was only in the book's concluding section that he made a single, simple reference to humanity when he wrote that eventually "light will be thrown on the origin of man and his history." Moreover, he never used the word evolution until February 1872 when the sixth and final edition of *Origin* was published.

After *The Origin of Species* was published, Darwin decided to continue his work, seeking additional and more compelling evidence in support of his theory of evolution by natural selection. Darwin devoted the balance of his life to researching and writing on a broad spectrum of biological topics.

He frequently worked on more than one project at a time. Given the ambitious schedule Darwin set for himself, he rarely left his home. When he did so, it generally was for very brief periods. He became more and more reclusive, working each day his health permitted, resting or seeking therapy if it did not. While he always graciously welcomed the company of visitors such as Hooker, Lyell, and Huxley, generally his only connection to the outside world was the enormous amount of correspondence he sent and received.

During the twenty-two years that followed the publication of *The Origin of Species*, Darwin wrote ten books, revised *The Origin of Species* five times, and completed several second editions of existing works. The new works presented new information and expanded upon existing evidence in support of natural selection.

For example, in *The Descent of Man and Selection in Relation to Sex* published in February 1871, Darwin illustrated how choosing a mate influenced the physical—and to a degree cultural—evolution of humanity. Factors such as a female's physical condition and beauty and a male's bodily strength and prowess as a hunter were features favorably influencing the selection of a mate. Those positive characteristics that influenced mate selection would then be passed on to the children of the sexual union and in the end be inherited by subsequent generations of humans thereby insuring the fitness and increasing the survivability of the human race. One interesting observation found in *The Descent of Man* is Darwin's contention that humanity did not evolve from existing species of simians but rather both ape and human shared a common ancestor. (Contemporary paleontologists share his view.)

With the aim of garnering additional support for his theory of species modification and adaptation, Darwin did extensive research on plant life. His books in that area included studies on orchids, insect-eating plants, climbing plants, flowering plants, movement in plants, and vegetable moulds. In *Insectivorous Plants* published in July 1875, he discussed, among others, the Venus flytrap, a plant he had studied that for years had fascinated him (*Insectivorous Plants*, a very popular book, outsold *The Origin of Species* on its first day of publication). He discovered that the plant's ability to trap insects was an adaptation permitting it to survive in an environment in which the ground provided few precious nutrients such as nitrogen for the plant's root system to absorb. In the absence of nourishment obtained from the earth itself, certain characteristics evolved which allowed the plant to obtain its nutrition from flying insects. From Darwin's perspective, one of nature's oddities could be explained by the process of natural selection and subsequent adaptation.

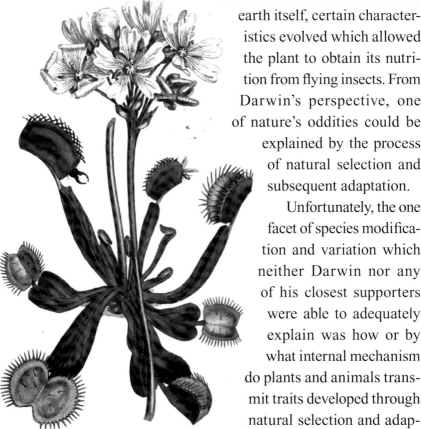

Darwin was fascinated by the Venus flytrap and studied it for years.

Unfortunately, the one facet of species modification and variation which neither Darwin nor any of his closest supporters were able to adequately explain was how or by what internal mechanism do plants and animals transmit traits developed through natural selection and adaptation? More specifically, what insures or guarantees that one generation of any species will inherit—and further guarantees that future generations will continue to inherit—favorable variations?

Darwin at first attempted to answer these questions with pangenesis, a process based upon the supposition that all living cells contain miniscule particles which he called gemmules. Gemmules, he believed, contained the "information" necessary to duplicate the part of the organism in which the gemmule was located. The inheritance of physical characteristics occurs when gemmules from throughout a plant or animal are picked up by the organism's circulatory system, flow to the reproductive organs, and are passed on to the next generation by the reproductive cells. Accordingly, as a result of sexual reproduction each parent contributes characteristics to the offspring of that sexual union.

However, there was an inherent problem with the concept of pangenesis that forced Darwin ultimately to abandon it. If both parents are contributing equal or nearly equal amounts of gemmules to the offspring, a blending of traits would occur. For example, a man with an unusually large nose mating with a woman with an exceptionally small nose would logically have a child whose nose size fell somewhere in between. Yet that kind of blending rarely occurred. There were countless times that Darwin even encountered examples of progeny possessing features which resembled neither parent. Moreover, when a favorable variation—larger size, greater strength, more speed, brighter colors—did by chance occur in one member of a sizable population of plants or animals, what would or could prevent that trait from being blended away in that population?

Darwin reluctantly admitted that science's ignorance of the laws of variation was great. In his *Autobiography*, he called pangenesis nothing more that a hypothesis he had formulated in his quest for the mechanism underlying inheritance.

At the same time that Darwin was unsuccessfully searching for the mechanism of inheritance, Gregor Mendel, an Austrian monk, had discovered the secret to inheritance (genetics) while conducting a series of experiments with the garden pea. Unfortunately Mendel, being neither a recognized scientist nor affiliated with any universities or scientific organizations, carried out his experiments unheralded and unnoticed. Darwin never learned of the new knowledge that would later come to underpin his theory.

Gregor Mendel and the Laws of Inheritance

Gregor Mendel (b. 1822), a quiet and gentle man, was an Augustinian monk whose interest in the natural sciences led him to conduct a series of experiments related to the subject of heredity. Mendel was attempting to understand the laws of inheritance, specifically, how physical characteristics are passed down from generation to generation and preserved in a population of plants and animals. Mendel's landmark experiment involved the garden pea and was conducted in a narrow, one hundred and twenty foot long patch of earth just outside the walls of his monastery in Bruun, Austria.

Mendel chose the common, edible garden pea for several reasons. It was both easy to plant and to pollinate. Moreover, individual plants were capable of germinating many times. Most important, the plants themselves were available with numerous contrasting traits such as tall

Gregor Mendel

and short stalks, round and wrinkled peas, green and yellow peas, flat and inflated pods, and several other characteristics. In 1856 Mendel began his experiments.

He decided to monitor seven contrasting traits as he cross-pollinated his pea plants. Carefully inspecting each successive generation, Mendel scrupulously noted the characteristics of each new lot of plants, indicating in his record book if any traits blended, were lost, or displayed anything unusual in nature. The first generation of hybrids (the mixture of round/wrinkled, tall/short, etc.) exhibited only one characteristic of the parent plants. For example, all of the round/wrinkled cross-pollinated plants produced only round peas. From this Mendel concluded that the traits that surfaced after the first crossbreeding were dominant (his term) and those that did not were recessive (again, his term). But when he crossed the hybrids, the wrinkled peas once again began surfacing. He rightly concluded that although they, the wrinkled peas, had skipped a generation, they had not been lost—somewhere within that first group of hybrids the wrinkled peas had managed to maintain their characteristics intact.

Mendel continued his cross-pollination experiment for nine years keeping an accurate account of the numbers and ratios of dominant and recessive traits that would successfully surface over the nine years. He discovered that the figures, especially the ratios, became predictable year after year causing him to deduce that a combination of mathematical and biological laws were obviously driving the process. He realized that some internal mechanism in the pea plants served as a regulatory factor in the breeding process and was the ultimate determinant of which features would breed and what the ratios of those features would be. For the length of his experiment, Mendel observed and documented nearly 13,000 individual hybrid specimens.

Mendel's study gave rise to his three laws of inheritance.

I. *Law of Independent Segregation:* All visible traits found in living things are maintained intact and independent of each other from generation to generation and do not blend when reproductively transmitted.

2. *Law of Independent Assortment:* Pairs of traits (round/wrinkled, tall/short, etc.) are transmitted independent of each other.

3. *Law of Dominance:* Where traits are paired, one will always be dominant and the other recessive.

Mendel's laws of inheritance explain that which Darwin was never able to discover, namely, why a favorable variation was not lost or "swamped" in a reproductively large group of organisms. (Since the rise of genetic science some of Mendel's conclusions have been modified, however they still provide the basic framework explaining how genetic inheritance operates.)

In February 1865 Mendel presented his work before the Brunn Society of the Study of Natural Science. The following year he published a monograph, *Experiments with Plant Hybrids,* explaining that hereditary factors do not blend but are passed intact from generation to generation. His work could have revolutionized science's ideas on heredity and probably legitimized Darwin's theory of natural selection (although Darwin was still alive he was unaware of Mendel's study). However neither his presentation nor his publication succeeded in arousing any interest among those who heard or read it.

In 1868 Gregor Mendel was made abbot of the monastery at Brunn. Because of the enormous amount of administrative responsibilities that came with his new position, Mendel had to suspend all further experiments on heredity. On January 6, 1884, the kindly monk died, beloved by the members of his monastic community and by those living in the nearby town whose lives he had touched, but a virtual unknown in the world of science.

In 1900, a Dutch botanist, Hugo de Vries, while puzzling over the question of inheritance, came upon Gregor Mendel's monograph, which he revealed to the world on March 24 of that year in a paper read before the German Botanical Society. By coincidence, later that year a German (Karl Correns) and an Austrian (Erich Tscher) botanist, both working independent of de Vries and each other, discovered and made public Mendel's work.

ten

Honors and Controversy

C harles Darwin's theory of evolution by natural selection, although widely admired for its extensive and persuasive documentation, was not immediately accepted by many members of the world's scientific community. Without an explanation for the mechanism underlying the inheritance of favorable variations, Darwin was never able to gain universal recognition for his ideas.

Despite so many scientists reluctance to accept the theory of natural selection, Darwin was still acknowledged as one of science's preeminent figures. Letters of praise for his work arrived almost daily at his home. He was continually invited to appear before many of England's and the world's leading scientific organizations. In 1864, the Royal Society awarded Darwin the Copley Medal, the highest honor it could bestow. While the medal was not specifically linked to the publication of *The Origin of Species*, it was awarded in recognition of his enormous contributions to science. He was the recipient of similar awards for the rest of his life, including an honorary LL.D (a doctorate of laws) from his alma mater Cambridge University and the celebrated Baly Medal of the Royal College of Physicians.

Darwin continued to be plagued by ill health. For one period early in the 1860s, he endured nearly thirty consecutive days of vomiting, which left him considerably weakened. Yet he still carried on with his research and managed to produce a substantial number of publications. In addition to his new scientific books and the numerous revisions of many of his earlier works, Darwin authored a biography of his grandfather entitled *Life of Erasmus Darwin* and his *Autobiography*. He also wrote 105 papers of varying lengths that appeared in numerous science publications.

The controversy sparked by *The Origin of Species* was dispiriting to Darwin, especially when the criticism was malicious. Given his physical condition and sensitive personality, he did not endure scorn well. Yet Darwin was fortunate in winning the loyalty of many friends, especially Hooker, Lyell, and Huxley. They always rushed to his aid with support and encouragement, eager to defend Darwin when his gentle demeanor left him without the resolve needed to confront his challengers.

In August 1881, Darwin received a telegram informing him that his brother Erasmus has died in London. He had always been close to his brother and was greatly disturbed by the death, and the emotional toll had an ill effect on Darwin's own health. For several years, he had been suffering from heart palpitations. After Erasmus's passing, his palpitations

PUNCH'S ALMANACK FOR 1882.

MAN·IS·BVT·A·WORM·

Darwin endured a great deal of criticism during his lifetime, much of it malicious. Caricatures such as this one ridiculed his theory of species evolution.

increased in frequency and were accompanied by chest pains. As a result of his heart ailment, he tired easily. The loss of vigor was soon followed by a loss of appetite. He found it progressively more difficult to engage in walking, writing, talking, or activity of any sort. Near the end of the third week of April 1882 he was weakened to the point where it appeared he did not have long to live. His doctors admitted to being powerless to help and his family was called in for twenty-four hour vigils.

A portrait of Darwin listening as Emma plays the piano. *(Courtesy of The London Art Archive/Alamy)*

On April 19, 1882, after lapsing in and out of consciousness several times, Charles Darwin died at 3:30 p.m., surrounded by children and held in the arms of his wife Emma. His family prepared to have him buried in the cemetery in Downe, but friends convinced the family that Darwin should be given a state burial within the walls of Westminster Abbey where many of England's most notable citizens were interred. Among his pall bearers were Thomas Henry Huxley, Joseph Dalton Hooker, and Alfred Russel Wallace.

The seven surviving Darwin children all outlived both their mother and father. Darwin had always wondered if Annie's premature death was the result of hereditary factors related to his marriage to Emma, his first cousin. He harbored

Darwin's funeral *(Courtesy of The Print Collector/Alamy)*

fears that what occurred to Annie could possibly happen to his other children. Darwin's fears were unfounded, though.

Each of the Darwin children kept the family name proud. William (1839-1914) became a prominent banker in Southampton, retiring to London in 1902 when his wife Sara died. Henrietta (1843-1930) became the family historian. Along with her husband Richard Litchfield, she collected and edited two lengthy volumes of family letters which were published as *Emma Darwin: A Century of Family Letters*. George (1845-1912) became a scientist and taught astronomy at Cambridge University; the majority of his research related to the evolution of the solar system. Elizabeth (1847-1926), the only one of the Darwin children who did not marry, lived with her mother. Known as Bessy, she was never employed, preferring instead to devote her time to working with local folk who were physically or economically disadvantaged.

Francis (1848-1925), like his father, was interested in natural history. In addition to authoring and editing *The Life and Letters of Charles Darwin*, he was a lecturer at the Cambridge Botany School. Leonard (1850-1943) entered the military service, serving for twenty years as an officer in the Royal Engineers. He later was elected to England's House of Parliament where he held a seat for three years. He was

Members of the Royal Engineers, which Darwin's son Leonard served in as an officer for twenty years. *(Courtesy of Lordprice Collection/Alamy)*

involved in public activities for most of his life. Although twice married, he had no children from either marriage. Horace (1851-1928) was a successful and prosperous businessman. He and his wife Ada had three children. Horace's daughter, Nora Barlow (1885-1989), was the editor of *The Autobiography of Charles Darwin*.

Emma left their home in Downe shortly after Charles's death. Purchasing a house called The Grove located near the center of Cambridge, she chose not to sell the family home in Downe. Bessy, Francis (a widower for six years), and Francis's six-year-old son Bernard joined Emma in Cambridge. Emma remained alert and active until she peacefully passed away in October 1896.

Emma was not buried beside Darwin as the family had always assumed would be the case. Instead, Darwin was buried with a group of England's most famous scientists. Entombed immediately to his right in Westminster Abbey was his friend John Herschel, whose book on *Natural Philosophy* exerted a pivotal influence upon Darwin's thinking. Beyond Herschel lay the remains of the most acclaimed scientist in human history, Sir Isaac Newton.

It was fitting that he was buried so near Newton. Darwin embodied the final stage of the scientific revolution that Newton and his predecessors Copernicus, Galileo, and Kepler helped to create. It was Newton who, in his *Principia Mathematica*, demonstrated through mathematics and empirical observation that the universe is governed by laws, not disordered impulse.

What Newton achieved in mapping out the laws and mechanisms driving the physical universe, Darwin's *Origin of Species* achieved for the world of biology. Since all living things sprang from the same fount and their development and survival was dependent upon the same laws of nature, it follows that all living things also were connected—from the microscopic amoeba to the mightiest of animals. Darwin gave life science an organizing principle.

Darwin's theory continues to be controversial. The confrontation between Thomas Huxley and Bishop Wilberforce at the 1860 meeting of the British Association for the Advancement of Science was a harbinger of the disputes to come. Although natural selection and all that relates to it are now firmly grounded in the canons of modern biology, unrelenting opposition still exists.

One of the most well-known events in the ongoing battle between what is historically referred to as fundamentalism versus scientific modernism was the Scopes Trial of August 1925. John T. Scopes, a teacher from Dayton, Tennessee, was brought to trial for teaching Charles Darwin's theory of evolution to his high school biology students. The teaching of evolution violated a Tennessee state law which mandated that in Tennessee public schools only divine creation could be presented by teachers as an explanation for the origin and development of life on earth.

When Scopes announced that the gifted and nationally acclaimed criminal defense lawyer Clarence Darrow would be defending him, the prosecution secured the services of an equally prominent attorney, William Jennings Bryan, a man who had run three times unsuccessfully for the presidency of the United States. The prospect of two of America's greatest legal minds facing off in court on so controversial an issue instantly turned the trial into a national media event. Journalists from throughout the U.S. and several foreign

Famed lawyer and politician William Jennings Bryan arguing for the prosecution during the Scopes Trial in 1925. *(Courtesy of Hulton Archive/ Getty Images)*

countries descended upon the little town of Dayton to witness the trial

Bryan, as the champion of fundamentalism, showed up in court each day with a King James Bible in hand. For every argument by Clarence Darrow supporting Darwin's theory of evolution or, at the very least, the right to teach evolution and similar scientific theories, Bryan would find a passage in his Bible to refute the defense attorney's claims. For his part, Darrow countered prosecution arguments with what he contended was credible scientific evidence. Although Scopes was ultimately found guilty, throughout the trial a much larger issue overshadowed the defendant's innocence or guilt: fundamentalist teachings versus those of modern biology.

Another school of thought that became a popular alternative to Darwinian evolution echoes the beliefs of Alfred Russel Wallace. Referred to as theistic evolution, this belief combines elements critical to both evolutionary theory and divine creationism. Theistic evolution acknowledges the essentials of evolution while declaring that God is the author of the evolutionary process; many religions today accept this God-driven concept of evolution.

As for Darwin, from his days as a divinity student at Cambridge to his final years, his religious beliefs, like his biological beliefs, evolved. He began his life fully accepting the precepts of the Anglican Church. It was shortly after his five-year passage on the *Beagle* that Darwin began experiencing what would be an ongoing transformation in his views on God and religion. Recognizing that nature lacked permanence, he concluded that change was not only a fact of existence but also the very essence of life. Nonetheless he still saw the divine as the prime mover in nature's functions.

Later, delving deeper and deeper into the subject of evolution, he began questioning the very existence of God, believing instead that the indifferent hand of chance directed all life. The tragedy of his daughter Annie's death in 1851 further contributed to his growing loss of faith. Soon after her death he confessed to being an agnostic. Coined by Thomas Huxley, the term refers to someone who claims that he or she does not know. But even then he vacillated. He once wrote to a friend "I think that generally . . . but not always, that an agnostic would be the most correct description of my state of mind." One of the last times he openly addressed the issue was in a letter to Joseph Hooker in 1870. By then, he had completely abandoned his original belief system.

> Your conclusion that all speculation about preordination is [an] idle waste of time is the only wise one; but how difficult it is not to speculate! My theology is a simple muddle; I cannot look at the universe as the result of blind chance yet I can see no evidence of beneficent design, or indeed of design of any kind, in the details.

In 1887, John Murray published *The Autobiography of Charles Darwin*, a chronological series of personal recollections Darwin had written over several years at the request of his children, as well as for his own enjoyment. The final pages of the *Autobiography* offer insights into the two faces of its author: the man and the scientist. He wrote that he lacked the wit and speed of apprehension that characterized more clever men like Thomas Huxley. Nor was he even moderately impressed by his powers to follow and understand abstract thought, claiming that he never would have been a successful metaphysician or mathematician. While he believed that his memory was extensive, he nonetheless thought it cloudy.

On a more favorable side however, he held that his powers of observation were above "the common run of men" and that he was always industrious in the collecting (both specimens and data) of those things he observed. More importantly, he noted that his love of nature remained "steady and ardent." In his reminisces he revealed a strong desire to understand and explain all that he observed and to combine these observations in categories of general laws. These traits, he believed, help explain his patience as he pondered difficult issues over long periods of time. Finally, he was convinced that his patience combined with his methodical work habits contributed enormously to his success as a scientist.

Darwin's final entry in his *Autobiography* was written on August 3, 1876. "With such moderate abilities as I possess," he wrote, "it is truly surprising that thus I should have influenced to a considerable extent the beliefs of scientific men on some important points."

Regardless of Darwin's modesty about his own abilities and influence, there is no doubt that he changed the way people viewed the world. For all of the controversy he inspired, Darwin sought only to truly understand nature, and share that joy with others. As he wrote in *The Origin of Species*: "When we no longer look at an organic being as a savage looks at ship, as at something wholly beyond his comprehension . . . how far more interesting . . . will the study of natural history become!"

Indeed, Darwin devoted his life to the study of nature and evolution because he felt it could benefit mankind and because he saw beauty and wonder in the idea that everything came from the same source but changed and grew more unique with time. "When I view all beings not as special creations, but as the lineal descendents of some few beings . . . they seem to me to become ennobled," he wrote in *The Origin of Species*. "There is grandeur in this view of life . . . that whilst this planet has gone cycling on according to the fixed law of gravity, from so simple a beginning endless forms most beautiful and most wonderful have been, and are being, evolved."

Timeline

1809	Born in Shrewsbury, England, on February 12.
1818	Enters Shrewsbury School.
1827	Admitted to Christ's College, Cambridge, to study for the clergy.
1831	Departs on five-year worldwide voyage aboard HMS *Beagle*.
1836	Returns to England and settles in Cambridge.
1837	Begins writing his first Notebook on the Transmutation of Species.
1839	Marries Emma Wedgewood, his first cousin.
1842	Publishes *Structure and Distribution of Coral Reefs*.
1844	Made vice president of the Geological Society.
1849	Elected to the Council of Royal Society.
1851	Publishes first monograph on barnacles; daughter Anne Elizabeth dies.
1853	Awarded Royal Society Medal for work on barnacles.
1859	*Origin of Species* published.

1872	Sixth edition of *Origin of Species* published.
1877	Receives honorary LL.D. from Cambridge University.
1879	Receives the Baly Medal of the Royal College of Physicians.
1882	Dies at home; receives state burial in Westminster Abbey.

Sources

CHAPTER ONE: An Unlikely Genius

p. 11, "You care for nothing . . ." Charles Darwin, *The Autobiography of Charles Darwin (1809-1882)* (New York: W. W. Norton & Company, 2005), 27.

p. 12, "this stupid fellow . . ." Gertrude Himmelfarb, *Darwin and the Darwinian Revolution* (Garden City: Doubleday and Company, 1962), 26.

p. 12, "when I left . . ." Darwin, *Autobiography*, 27.

p. 16, "on tearing off some old bark . . ." Ibid., 53.

p. 18, "the school as a means . . ." Ibid., 26.

p. 19, "a keen interest in the work," Ibid., 41.

p. 20, "the instruction at Edinburgh . . ." Ibid.

p. 20, "lectures on Materia Medica . . ." 47.

p. 20, "made his lectures . . ." Ibid.

p. 21-22, "I had scruples about . . ." Ibid., 49.

p. 23, "the strict and literal . . ." Ibid.

p. 23, "I had actually forgotten . . ." Ibid., 50.

CHAPTER TWO: The Making of a Scientist

p. 24, "during the three years . . ." Darwin, *Autobiography*, 50.

p. 24, "repugnant," Ibid.

p. 25, "The careful study . . ." Ibid., 51.

p. 28, "used to take his pupils . . ." 60.

p. 28, "the great men . . ." Leonard Jenyns, *Memoir of the Reverend John Stevens Henslow* (London: Van Voorst, 1862), Cambridge University Web site, "The Complete Works of Charles Darwin Online," http://Darwinonline.org.uk/content/frameset?viewtype=side&itemID=F830&pageseq=2.

p. 28, "The most perfect man . . . Francis Darwin, ed., *The*

Life and Letters of Charles Darwin, Vol. I (New York: Basic Books, 1959), 158.

p. 29, "the man who walks with Henslow," Ibid.

p. 29, "Hitherto I have never . . ." Himmelfarb, *Darwin*, 41.

p. 31, "Dr. Whewell was one . . ." Darwin, *Autobiography*, 56.

p. 32, "the greatest scientific . . . Francis Darwin, *The Life and Letters of Charles Darwin,* Vol. II, 422.

p. 33, "stirred up in me . . ." Ibid., 57.

p. 34, "that science consists . . ." Ibid., 59.

CHAPTER THREE: Aboard the *Beagle*

p. 38, "disreputable to . . ." Darwin, *Autobiography*, 192.

p. 39-40, "if it had not been . . ." Frederick Burkhardt, ed., *Charles Darwin's Letters: A Selection 1825-1859* (Great Britain: Cambridge University Press, 1996), 11.

p. 41, "the undertaking would be . . ." Ibid., 13.

p. 41, "If you can find . . ." Darwin, *Autobiography*, 60.

p. 42, "the most miserable . . ." Ibid., 66.

p. 45, "The misery I [have] endured. . ." Francis Darwin, *The Life and Letters of Charles Darwin,* Vol. I, 200.

p. 45, "everything that is delightful . . ." Ibid., 178.

p. 45, "It is no use . . ." Ibid., 181.

p. 46, "hot coffee," Darwin, *Autobiography*, 62.

CHAPTER FOUR: A Voyage of Discovery

p. 52, "The natural history . . ." Mark Ridley, ed., *The Darwin Reader* (New York: W. W. Norton & Company, 2006), 50.

p. 54, "of the infinite superiority . . ." Ibid., 7.

p. 55, "I always feel . . ." Himmelfarb, *Darwin*, 97.

p. 55, "I felt a high . . ." Darwin, *Autobiography*, 88.

p. 56, "zigzag manner of proceeding . . ." Burkhardt, *Charles Darwin's Letters*, 52.

CHAPTER FIVE: The Return Home
p. 59, "leading scientific men," Darwin, *Autobiography*, 68.
p. 63, "The success of my . . ." Ibid., 96.
p. 66, "Tears still sometimes come . . ." Ibid., 81.

CHAPTER SIX: The Theory of Evolution
p. 73, "no one definition . . ." Duncan M. Porter and Peter
   W. Graham, eds., *The Portable Darwin* (New York:
   Penguin Books, 1993), 136.
p. 73, "to define the undefinable," Francis Darwin, *The
   Life and Letters of Charles Darwin,* Vol. II, 88.
p. 76, "In July opened . . ." Gavin de Beer, *Charles
   Darwin* (Garden City: Doubleday and Company, 1967), 86.
p. 80, "fifteen months after . . ." Darwin, *Autobiography*, 98.
p. 81, Charles Darwin, *The Origin of Species byMeans
   of Natural Selection* (Chicago: Encyclopedia Britannica,
   1952), 33, 40.
p. 82, "How extremely stupid . . ." Rebecca Stefoff,
   Charles Darwin and the Evolution Revolution (New
   York: Oxford University Press, 1996), 89.
p. 83, "among Divines and Philosophers . . ." Loren
   Eiseley, *The Firmament of Time* (New York:
   Atheneum, 1984), 35.
p. 83, "such is the economy . . ." Ibid., 35,36.

CHAPTER SEVEN: A Cautious Scientist
p. 91, "pleased with the extreme . . ." Darwin,
   Autobiography, 94.
p. 94, "He rose early . . ." Michael White and John Gribbin,
   Darwin: A Life in Science (New York: Dutton, 1995), 260.
p. 95, "Few persons can have lived . . ." Darwin,
   Autobiography, 94-95.

CHAPTER EIGHT: *The Origin of Species*
p. 98, "one of my best friends . . ." Darwin,
   Autobiography, 87.

p. 100, "Besides a general interest . . ." Burkhardt,
Charles Darwin's Letters, 80.

p. 103, "that barnacles are conical . . ." Ibid., 107.

p. 105, "Well, which is the most . . ." Clark, *The Survival,* 100.

p. 108, "the more frequent . . ." J. A. Hammerton, ed.,
Outline of Great Books (New York: Wise & Company,
1937), 407.

p. 109, "permanent disuse of an organ . . ." Ibid., 407.

p. 112, "He (Wallace) has to day . . ." Burkhardt,
Charles Darwin's Letters, 188.

p. 112, "There is nothing . . ." Ibid., 189.

p. 114, "not, indeed, been marked . . ." White, *Darwin,* 210.

CHAPTER NINE: The Aftermath of *Origin*

p. 123-124, "If I would rather . . ." Janet Browne, *Charles
Darwin: The Power of Place* (Princeton: Princeton
University Press, 2002), 122.

p. 127, "light will be thrown . . ." Charles Darwin, *The
Origin of Species* (New York: Barnes & Noble Classics,
2004), 383.

CHAPTER TEN: Honors and Controversy

p. 145, "I think that generally . . ." Adrian Desmond &
James Moore, *Darwin* (New York: Warner Books,
1992), 636.

p. 146, "Your conclusion that all . . ." Darwin,
Autobiography, 130.

p. 146, "The common run of men," Ibid., 114.

p. 146, "Steady and ardent," Ibid., 115.

p. 147, "With such moderate abilities . . ." Ibid., 118.

p. 147, "When we no longer look . . ." Darwin, *The Origin
of Species,* 381.

p. 147, "When I view all beings . . ." Ibid., 383-384.

Bibliography

Appleman, Philip, ed. *Darwin*. New York: W. W. Norton & Company, 1979.

Behe, Michael J. *Darwin's Black Box: The Biochemical Challenge to Evolution*. New York: The Free Press, 1996.

———. *The Edge of Evolution: The Search for the Limits of Darwinism*. New York: Free Press, 2007.

Blackmore, Vernon, and Andrew Page. *Evolution, The Great Debate*. Oxford: Lion Publishing, 1989.

Bowlby, John. *Charles Darwin: A New Life*. New York: W. W. Norton & Company, 1991.

Brent, Peter. *Charles Darwin: A Man of Enlarged Curiosity*. New York: Harper & Row Publishers, 1981.

Browne, Janet. *Charles Darwin: The Power of Place*. Princeton: Princeton University Press, 2002.

———. *Charles Darwin: Voyaging*. Princeton: Princeton University Press, 1995.

Burkhardt, Frederick, ed. *Charles Darwin's Letters: A Selection 1825-1859*. Great Britain: Cambridge University Press, 1996.

Clark, Ronald W. *The Survival of Charles Darwin: A Biography of a Man and an Idea*. New York: Avon Books, 1986.

Darwin, Charles. *The Autobiography of Charles Darwin (1809-1882)*. New York: W. W. Norton & Company, 2005.

———. *The Expression of the Emotions in Man and Animals*. New York: Oxford University Press, 1998.

———. *The Illustrated Origin of Species*. Abridged and introduced by Richard E. Leakey. New York: Hill and Wang, 1979.

————. *The Origin of Species*. New York: Barnes & Noble Classics, 2004.

Darwin, Francis, ed. *The Life and Letters of Charles Darwin*, Volumes I & II. New York: Basic Books, 1959

Dawkins, Richard. *Climbing Mount Improbable*. New York: W. W. Norton & Company, 1997.

————. *The Blind Watchmaker: Why the Evidence of Evolution Reveals a Universe without Design*. New York: W. W. Norton & Company, 1987.

————. *The Selfish Gene*. New York: Oxford University Press, 1989.

de Beer, Gavin. *Charles Darwin*. Garden City: Doubleday and Company, 1967.

Dennett, Daniel C. *Darwin's Dangerous Idea: Evolution and the Meanings of Life*. New York: Simon and Schuster, 1995.

Desmond, Adrian, and James Moore. *Darwin*. New York: Warner Books, Inc., 1992.

Dixon, Bernard, ed. *From Creation to Chaos: Classic Writings in Science*. Oxford, England: Basil Blackwell, Ltd., 1989.

Eiseley, Loren. *Darwin's Century: Evolution and the Men Who Discovered It*. Garden City: Doubleday and Company, 1958.

Eldredge, Niles. *Darwin: Discovering the Tree of Life*. New York: W. W. Norton & Company, 2005.

Farrington, Benjamin. *What Darwin Really Said*. New York: Schocken Books, 1966.

Gould, Stephen Jay. *Ever Since Darwin: Reflections in Natural History*. New York: W. Norton & Company, 1979.

Haldane, J. B. S. *The Causes of Evolution*. Princeton: Princeton University Press, 1993.

Himmelfarb, Gertrude. *Darwin and the Darwinian*

Revolution. Garden City: Doubleday and Company, 1962.

Howard, Jonathan. *Darwin: A Very Short Introduction.* New York: Oxford University Press, 2001.

Johnson, Phillip E. *Darwin on Trial.* Downers Grove: InterVarsity Press, 1993.

Macbeth, Norman. *Darwin Retried.* New York: Dell Publishing Company, 1971.

Mayr, Ernst. *One Long Argument: Charles Darwin and the Genesis of Modern Evolutionary Thought.* Cambridge: Harvard University Press, 1991.

———. *What Evolution Is.* New York: Basic Books, 2001.

Moorehead, Alan. *Darwin and the Beagle.* New York: Penguin Books, 1971.

Morris, Richard. *The Evolutionists: The Struggle for Darwin's Soul.* New York: Henry Holt & Company, 2002.

Porter, Duncan M., and Peter W. Graham, eds. *The Portable Darwin.* New York: Penguin Books, 1993.

Quammen, David. *The Reluctant Mr. Darwin: An Intimate Portrait of Charles Darwin and the Making of His Theory of Evolution.* New York: W. W. Norton & Company, 2006.

Ridley, Mark, ed. *The Darwin Reader.* New York: W. W. Norton & Company, 1987.

Stefoff, Rebecca. *Charles Darwin and the Evolution Revolution.* New York: Oxford University Press, 1996.

Weiner, Jonathan. *The Beak of the Finch: A Story of Evolution in Our Time.* New York: Alfred A. Knopf, 1994.

White, Michael, and John Gribbin. *Darwin: A Life in Science.* New York: Dutton, 1995.

Zimmer, Carl. *Evolution: The Triumph of an Idea.* New York: HarperCollins Publishers, 2001.

Web sites

http://darwin-online.org.uk/
To learn practically everything there is to know about Charles Darwin, visit Cambridge University's "The Complete Works of Charles Darwin online." Here, visitors will find Darwin's complete publications, 20,000 private papers, extensive bibliography, manuscript catalogue, and hundreds of supplementary works, in addition to more than one thousand illustrations from Darwin's books and links to free audio mp3 files of Darwin's works.

http://www.darwinfoundation.org/
Web site of The Charles Darwin Foundation for the Galapagos Islands offers information about the foundation, established to help protect the Galapagos and educate people about the islands.

http://www.pbs.org/evolution
A video of Darwin and his "dangerous idea" are featured on this site, along with other articles and videos on the subject of evolution.

http://www.darwinproject.ac.uk/
Charles Darwin exchanged letters with nearly 2,000 people during his lifetime, and you can read many of those letters here on the Web site of the Darwin Correspondence Project.

Index